Shakespeare and Directing in Practice

*Shakespeare in Practice*

Series Editors:

**Stuart Hampton-Reeves**, Professor of Research-informed Teaching, University of Central Lancashire, UK, and Head of the British Shakespeare Association

**Bridget Escolme**, Reader in Drama, Queen Mary, University of London, UK

*Published:*

Andrew James Hartley
SHAKESPEARE AND POLITICAL THEATRE IN PRACTICE

Terri Power
SHAKESPEARE AND GENDER IN PRACTICE

Stephen Purcell
SHAKESPEARE AND AUDIENCE IN PRACTICE

Darren Tunstall
SHAKESPEARE AND GESTURE IN PRACTICE

*Forthcoming:*

Bridget Escolme
SHAKESPEARE AND COSTUME IN PRACTICE

Alexa Joubin
SHAKESPEARE AND DIASPORA IN PRACTICE

Kathryn Prince
SHAKESPEARE AND EMOTIONS IN PRACTICE

Don Weingust
SHAKESPEARE AND ORIGINAL PRACTICES

---

Shakespeare in Practice
Series standing order
ISBN 978–0–230–27637–6 hardcover
ISBN 978–0–230–27638–3 paperback
(*outside North America only*)

You can receive future titles in this series as they are published by placing a standing order. Please contact your bookseller or, in case of difficulty, write to us at the address below with your name and address, the title of the series and the ISBN quoted above.

Customer Services Department, Macmillan Distribution Ltd, Houndmills, Basingstoke, Hampshire RG21 6XS, England

# Shakespeare and Directing in Practice

1st edition

Kevin Ewert

© Kevin Ewert, under exclusive licence to Macmillan Publishers Ltd, part of Springer Nature 2018

All rights reserved. No reproduction, copy or transmission of this publication may be made without written permission.

No portion of this publication may be reproduced, copied or transmitted save with written permission or in accordance with the provisions of the Copyright, Designs and Patents Act 1988, or under the terms of any licence permitting limited copying issued by the Copyright Licensing Agency, Saffron House, 6–10 Kirby Street, London EC1N 8TS.

Any person who does any unauthorized act in relation to this publication may be liable to criminal prosecution and civil claims for damages.

The author has asserted his right to be identified as the author of this work in accordance with the Copyright, Designs and Patents Act 1988.

First published 2018 by
PALGRAVE

Palgrave in the UK is an imprint of Macmillan Publishers Limited, registered in England, company number 785998, of 4 Crinan Street, London N1 9XW.

Palgrave® and Macmillan® are registered trademarks in the United States, the United Kingdom, Europe and other countries.

ISBN 978-1-137-36929-1 hardback
ISBN 978-1-137-36928-4 paperback

This book is printed on paper suitable for recycling and made from fully managed and sustained forest sources. Logging, pulping and manufacturing processes are expected to conform to the environmental regulations of the country of origin.

A catalogue record for this book is available from the British Library.

A catalog record for this book is available from the Library of Congress.

# Contents

| | |
|---|---|
| *Series Editors' Preface* | vi |
| *Author Preface* | ix |
| Introduction | 1 |
| **Part I  In Theory** | **17** |
| 1  The Play's the Thing | 19 |
| 2  The Thing is the Thing | 29 |
| **Part II  In Practice** | **49** |
| 3  The Production Machine | 51 |
| 4  Playing with Time and Space | 63 |
| 5  Devising Shakespeare | 80 |
| 6  Fixing Shakespeare | 91 |
| 7  My Year of Shakespeare | 107 |
| **Part III  Provocation and Debate** | **131** |
| 8  A Conversation with Rude Mechs | 133 |
| *Annotated Reading List* | 144 |
| *Bibliography* | 148 |
| *Index* | 152 |

# Series Editors' Preface

The books in the *Shakespeare in Practice* series chart new directions for a performance approach to Shakespeare. They represent the diverse and exciting work being undertaken by a new generation of Shakespeareans who have either come to the field from theatre practice or have developed a career that combines academic work with performing, directing or dramaturgy. Many of these authors are based in drama departments and use practical workshops for both teaching and research. They are conversant with the fields of English literature and performance studies, and they move freely between them. This series gives them an opportunity to explore both fields and to lend greater prominence to some of the key questions that occupy performance studies in the study of Shakespeare.

We intend this series to shape the way in which Shakespeare in performance is taught and researched. Our authors approach performance as a creative practice and a work of art in its own right. We want to create a new curriculum for Shakespeare in performance, which embraces the full complexity of the art of theatre and is underpinned by performance theory.

The first part of each book explores the theoretical issues at stake, often drawing on key works in performance studies as well as seminal writings by theatre practitioners. The second part consists of a series of critical studies of performance in practice, drawing on theatre history but chiefly focusing on contemporary productions and practitioners. Finally, we have asked all of our authors to engage in a debate with another scholar or practitioner so that each book ends with an engaging and unresolved debate.

All of our books draw on a wide range of plays so that teachers can choose which they want to focus on. There will be no volume on *Hamlet*, *A Midsummer Night's Dream* or *Romeo and Juliet* – every volume can be used as a model for every play in the canon. Similarly, none of the books exhaust the research possibilities that they open: there is more, much more, work to be done on every topic in this series.

The first book in the series is by Stephen Purcell on *Shakespeare and the Audience in Practice*. Studies of Shakespeare in performance often leave aside the audience. Either the critic's own response is used to voice the audience, or the audience is effaced altogether. Questions about the role of the audience in constructing the theatrical event are often posed, but rarely answered, at conferences and seminars. Leaving the audience out of theatrical analysis is problematic, but including them is, if anything, even more problematic. How does one give voice to an audience? Is an audience exterior to the performance, or is it part of it – in which case, it is possible to 'read' the audience in a critical way? What research tools do we need to conduct such work? Or is the audience an illusion? Purcell addresses how notions of audience, audience configuration, audience expectation and audiences as they figure in play texts all produce meaning in the theatre. His work is the ideal book with which to begin this series.

For the second book, Andrew James Hartley offers a timely overview of *Shakespeare and Political Theatre in Practice*. The development of political theatre in the twentieth century has had a profound influence on the performance of Shakespeare's work. In a sense, Shakespeare's theatre has always been a political one which is keenly aware of its context. His earliest plays vividly dramatize the power games at the heart of England's bloody civil wars in the fifteenth century, and throughout his career Shakespeare returned again and again to critical questions of authority, identity and transgression. This is one of the reasons why Bertolt Brecht studied the Elizabethan theatre, among other forms, when developing the 'alienation' effect for his own highly politicized theatre. One of the consequences of Brecht's work, together with that of many other innovators from the last century, is that we can no longer approach Shakespeare performance in a neutral way. Hartley's study is an important contribution to the series which demonstrates the potency (and the danger) of politicizing Shakespeare in performance.

Terri Power's volume on *Shakespeare and Gender in Practice* presents new research and new thinking on one of the most important debates in current theatre studies. The performance of gender in Shakespeare's plays has been a richly studied topic in theatre studies, English literary studies and early modern scholarship. However, despite Shakespeare's diverse narrative profile of multiculturalism and his inclusive 'humanist' appeal, when it comes to gender in casting and playing, Shakespeare production often follows familiar, normative patterns. Power's examination of Shakespeare and gender challenges 'traditional' notions of casting and character through an intersectional feminist study of current Shakespeare in practice. The book explores questions of gender construction and performance arising from all-male 'original practices' productions of Shakespeare and all-female versions; challenges the stigma still attached to transvestism and cross-gender performance; offers new perspectives on how early modern attitudes to gender are dealt with in contemporary production; and considers broader issues around the terminologies, documentation and resources that might enable artists and scholars to archive and develop new challenges for Shakespeare audiences in the performance of gender.

Questions about the body and how the actor uses it to create (and subvert) theatrical meaning are at the centre of the next book in the series, Darren Tunstall's *Shakespeare and Gesture in Practice*. How does the actor's body make meaning in collaboration with Shakespeare? It is perhaps easy to assume that there is a paucity of evidence about the kinds of gestures actors might have used in Shakespeare's theatre – and to assume that what actors do now might be comparably less 'formal', more 'natural'. Tunstall's book offers the reader a history of gesture in rhetoric and performance: a history that sheds new light on what the acting of Shakespeare's plays might have looked at in the past. Through accounts of recent performance and interviews with practitioners, the book then explores how actors both find and use gestural language in Shakespeare performance today. The book historicizes Shakespeare's gestural languages and explores the ways in which theatre practices have imposed their own gestural languages upon them. Thus the reader is prepared for an exciting new perspective on contemporary theatre's approaches to Shakespeare, asking how we make meaning from Shakespeare through the body.

Kevin Ewert's *Shakespeare and Directing in Practice* is a personal and provocative look at the figure of the director. Since the millennium, forms of immersive and 'non-directed' Shakespeare have challenged the primacy of the director in theatrical creation, yet, as Ewert says in his Introduction, in most cases the director remains the central figure in any production, the person to whom we most readily attribute its vision and achievement. Ewert traces different models of the director, from what he calls the 'glorified manager' to some sort of guru. The questions that Ewert poses for himself, and for us, are important ones: what is the purpose of a director? Does theatre need directing? And how do directors, through their practice, shape our current understanding of Shakespeare and his relevance to our times? However, Ewert's focus is not on the director as an individual but on the practice of directing, which may belong to one person in a company or to many. Ewert's case studies present innovative and daring approaches that put pressure on Shakespeare as a textual authority and on traditional modes of performance. As an experienced director himself, Ewert is able to draw on his own experience to provide insights into the directing process.

Stuart Hampton-Reeves<br>Bridget Escolme

# Author Preface

Write what you know, or make things up? The main character of Martin McDonagh's *The Pillowman* has some interesting things to say about that writer's dilemma, which his practice appears to delightfully contradict. Perhaps that's how it should be. For this book, I've tried to write what I know, which has come about through a 30-odd-year adventure of making things up, in countless rehearsal rooms and with many wonderful co-conspirators.

Many thanks: to the University of Pittsburgh at Bradford for faculty research grants and course releases in support of work on this book; to the *Shakespeare in Practice* Series Editors Stuart Hampton-Reeves and Bridget Escolme for the opportunity, and to Stuart for detailed and helpful feedback along the way; to all the people who have worked with me to make some theatre, and whose creativity and insights inform every aspect of what I've come to understand about directing; to Jaybird O'Berski, fellow adventurer; and to Kelley, Peter and Eliot for much love and even more patience.

# Introduction

In the spring of 2015 the off-Broadway company Bedlam presented two Shakespeare productions in repertory. The trick was that the two productions were of the exact same script. The artistic director, Eric Tucker, explained:

> The version we're calling *Twelfth Night or What You Will* centers around the theme that love can be difficult and extremely hard but in the end also very magical and rewarding ... Our other version, which we're calling *What You Will or Twelfth Night*, centers around the theme that love is absolutely maddening and doesn't always turn out okay in the end but it's a wild ride.
>
> (Healy 2015)

This was some clever, buzzworthy marketing, and both productions – listed separately – were Critic's Picks in *The New York Times*. Same script, different approaches: a theatrical banality, were it not for the simultaneity and the inspired/tortured logistics of two separate productions of the same script by the same company with the same actors and same director in rep under two different names. Promotional genius? Perhaps. At the same time, something about the two titles gestures towards a crux of both surface nomenclature and underlying theory in the very practical world of theatre-making. Guiding idea, central theme, production concept: anyone who goes to the theatre on a regular basis gets it, and by 'it' we probably just mean 'directing'. But the two titles beg a greater question about scripts and productions and the director function that in some way mediates between them. We address that question with words that speak to our comfort level, our conservatism or otherwise, with what theatre people get up to when they try to make some new art that has an old script in it. Two themes. Two versions. Two interpretations. Two visions. Two productions. But *Twelfth Night or What You Will/What You Will or Twelfth Night* comes out and says the sacrilegious, or maybe just the obvious: concept be damned – two different ways really means two different plays.

In many ways, the director has become the central figure of the modern theatre – the person whose work, though at times the least directly visible, can eclipse the writer's and the actor's as the driving force in the theatrical event. While directorial functions have been around as long as the theatre itself, the director as single centralized focal point of (aesthetic) power and authority is a fairly recent phenomenon. There are many ways this power can be used in the theatre, in pre-planning, in rehearsal, leading up to public performance and beyond. There are also specific implications to this power being brought to bear on a script by Shakespeare.

A director works in words, images and ideas, but not in some abstract sense. Robert Lepage says that we make theatre to confirm intuition, and Peter Brook (1988, 3) says he begins his work from a formless hunch – but intuitions and hunches must be embodied in the theatre, *in action*, in time and space. To confirm intuition and give form to a hunch, a director works with actors and designers, for a company and sometimes as the leader of his or her own company, sometimes directly with a playwright and most often with some kind of pre-existing text. But what does a director do, and how does he or she do it, in this communal drive towards action? Is the director a glorified manager? A taskmaster? A collaborator? A curator? An irreverent instigator and then a rigorous editor? A guru and a visionary? An innovator or, more specifically (and problematically), *the* innovator? Along with how (the craft, the skill sets), we need to ask why: why does the theatre need a director? What is a director for, exactly? The how and the why, the what and the what for of directing are the subjects of this book. The theory is drawn from the modern theatre and a variety of contemporary approaches. The test cases are mostly Shakespearean.

***Trust Us, This Is All Made Up*, or, The Director Function in Real Time and a Theory To Go With It**: First, the what: what is directing? I'm a fan of the counter-intuitive gesture, and so when I teach directing to my students I start by showing them something that doesn't actually have a director or a script. They aren't tempted to get hung up on individual personality in action – oh, that's how she/he does it! – or on thematic preconceptions – that's not how I see this play! Instead, they can just look at the director function in action. Whatever a *director* might look like – and we come in all shapes and sizes and expressive dimensions – this is what *directing* looks like.

TJ Jagodowski and David Pasquesi are Chicago actors who specialize in long-form improv. Together they take to the stage with nothing, and with nothing planned, and an hour or so later wrap up a detailed, vividly imagined, multi-character, narrative-driven piece of theatre that they will never perform again. One of these pieces is at the centre of the 2009 documentary *Trust Us, This Is All Made Up* (dir. Alex Karpovsky), and it starts about 18½ minutes into the film. The lights come up in the Barrow Street Theatre in New York on two guys in nondescript street clothes with three chairs on an otherwise bare stage. They look at each other. After about 20 seconds one of them speaks. After another three minutes or so a detail drops that focuses things and drives the characters and story through to the end some 52 minutes later. It is not a skit, it is not a sketch, it is a fully realized, compelling, hilarious, memorable story, well-told. I let my students watch it through, and then I make them watch it again to try to figure out how that just happened.

TJ and Dave take to the stage with 'nothing' – but only if you understand 'something' in the theatre to mean on the one hand sets and costumes and on the other a script that is supplying the dialogue and characters and incidents etc. Like Cordelia's 'nothing' there is a lot more to it. I try to get my students to see how incredibly full the first few minutes of this piece actually are, and to identify the many specific theatrical elements that are in play. There are two bodies, occupying space, with exactitude. There is stillness, but it is a fully inhabited stillness. This inhabited stillness creates tension in the space and between the characters, tension because something, perhaps something big, has just happened. Then a gesture emerges: there is a slow nod. That gesture seems to generate emotional content in an accompanying facial expression, a distinct look of sympathy and support. The look eventually generates a line: 'You'll bounce back, man.' That little bit of sympathy establishes a protagonist in crisis and an observer of that crisis – a sidekick? A Sancho Panza? Little details start to emerge in small talk, personalities develop based on that initial look, an instigating incident becomes apparent (if not yet its cause, content or effect) and an offstage antagonist is established and reacted to. 'Narrative' emerges in a fairly traditional way as dialogue accumulates, but it does so in the context of what looks and feels like – is – clear and careful *direction*: exquisitely modulated pacing, visual focus and variation, charged silences and sudden rushes of feeling, vocal styling that is distinctive and differentiated, idiosyncratic line deliveries, detailed attention to gesture and physical shapes, a clear floor pattern delineating multiple spaces and facilitating the additions, entrances or revelations of further characters in different locations, etc. etc. etc.

And so I ask my students to look carefully at all the elements of direction in this piece that has no director. I encourage them to consider ways of handling text from this play that doesn't have a script. I suggest they extrapolate rehearsal methods from a performance that isn't rehearsed. I do this because there is rigorous methodology on display, with a simple philosophy – a theory – that is driving how it happens. It is first principles stuff, but the kind of stuff that both beginner actors infatuated with improv games and experienced directors of supposedly rock-solid scripts have a habit of ignoring. As Pasquesi puts it in the documentary, 'If you pay attention instead of trying to make stuff up, everything's already there.' It's a methodology based on patience – nothing needs to be forced since something is always happening – and on decisiveness – if you are attentive to what is already happening, you'll know what to do and when to do it. Pasquesi thinks of it as a kind of directing without dictating:

> If we force our ideas into it, then we spend the rest of the time justifying it which is not exploring anymore ... that's why we walk out kind of empty, to be available to anything that might be there, rather than 'my great ideas.'

Yes, the actors are directing themselves, and they are doing it from within a show they are, in real time, making up. But they are doing it with qualities that I would argue any director needs. By being wholly attuned to what is going on in the room, they are *open to* and are *generating* constant stimuli and provocations, which they then deftly, simply, ingeniously handle, in bold and satisfyingly theatrical ways.

Of course, an example that utilizes a couple of comparative brain surgeons in long-form improv must yield, somewhat, in the face of the cold, hard fact of a script by Shakespeare. A Shakespeare script is a lot to bring into the room, with its particular theatrical challenges and opportunities and cultural baggage. But what is it? What is it really? Does it require, or just attract, certain ways of directing? Is it possible for a director to be available and pay attention to – or to prioritize – anything else when Shakespeare is in the room?

**Two Trains Running:** The 2012 collaboration between The Wooster Group and the Royal Shakespeare Company on *Troilus and Cressida* – with The Wooster Group actors (directed by Elizabeth LeCompte) playing the Trojans as ersatz Native North Americans sprouting spray-painted Styrofoam statuary and often moving in synch with an eclectic variety of film clips, and the RSC actors (directed by Mark Ravenhill) playing the Greeks as sometimes loud, sometimes camp but generally recognizable modern soldiers – offers a fascinating case study where radically different notions of the relationship between text and performance were bundled into one strange hybrid creation. Not surprisingly, this was a production with defenders and detractors.

This defence and detraction rather neatly unsplices the collaborative efforts (if they could even be called that) along an obvious aesthetic faultline of differing priorities – priorities both on display from the practitioners and revealed in audience responses. Paul Prescott's and Andrew Cowie's takes on the show posted on bloggingshakespeare.com outline some of the important issues. Prescott characterized it as a train wreck (Prescott 2012), and perhaps having two trains – two casts, two companies, two directors, two rehearsal periods mostly in two different countries – running at each other in one production could not have resulted in anything else. But the trainwreck analogy might imply that there is some sort of solid Shakespearean track – 'the play', if you like – from which this production spectacularly derailed. Alternately, Cowie suggests we might need to look carefully at priorities and process (the working methodologies rather than interpretive intentions) in order to come to any useful assessment of the results of this particular experiment (Cowie 2012). Cowie asks: is a production meant to explain and illustrate 'the play' or is it a response to it, and therefore always a new work in its own right?

For me, this argument hearkened back to a seminal moment from another country and century. After I finished my undergraduate degree, I spent a number of years in Toronto failing to become an actor and thinking about maybe being a director. So, when the World Stage Festival at Harbourfront in 1988 held a two-week 11-session round-table forum, 'About Directing', to accompany the official performance programme – and it was free – I attended as many as I could. I still have the file folder with my hastily scrawled notes, peppered with stars and arrows and feverish underlinings to mark the most important ideas: like Lev Dodin of the Maly Theatre talking about how an ensemble company should have a 'common soul' and how the key to theatre lies in what you don't know; like Mladen Materic of the former Yugoslavia's Open Stage talking about text vs body and language vs movement in the theatre, and how a director has to decide for him- or herself which comes first and what is the most important, and how for Materic it is both – text isn't bad, movement isn't best, he doesn't elevate one at the expense of the other but sees how they can exist complementarily in the best way possible; and like Robert Lepage talking about making theatre from 'sensible resources' – working from a sensation, an emotion, a colour, an object, a piece of music that you don't necessarily know the meaning of but realize that there is a lot of 'something' in, and how directing company-created work is about moving from rich obscurity towards more cohesive themes and ideas.

Very heady stuff, but for me the real take-away of the whole festival, and the biggest buzz that its events generated that I can recall, wasn't in the forum or on the stage but centred around a review of one of the shows. In my file I still have the clipping, a carefully folded yellowing talisman of something that I knew was important at the time even if I didn't wholly understand why. The show was Heiner Müller's *Hamletmachine*, the company was the Quebec group Carbone 14, the director was Gilles Maheu, and the review was by Ray Conlogue, the theatre critic for *The Globe and Mail*, which is English Canada's equivalent of *The New York Times* or *The Guardian*. The show arrived at the Festival with a lot of hype – so much, and so persuasive, that it was the only production I collected my scarce pennies to go and see. I liked the show; Conlogue hated it – but his review really smacked me in the face with the bigger theatrical/theoretical question of 'what we are doing here?' Conlogue appreciated Maheu's 'command of stage imagery' and commended the 'physical discipline' of all the performers, but ultimately director and performers, imagery and physicality, served only to 'distract the viewer from wondering whether they are communicating anything either of Shakespeare or Muller' (Conlogue 1988):

> Take the celebrated set-piece in the middle of the show where the German Hamlet (Rodrigue Proteau) and one of the Ophelias (Johane Madore) do a terrifying dance using a large electric fan as a prop. It is weighted in such a way that either dancer can sprawl over the fan without crashing ignominiously to the floor, even as the fan is hauled around the stage by the other dancer. To add further visual interest, the fan is plugged in, so that we have billowing skirts and hair as well.
>
> There is no denying the effect is drastic and overwhelming. But is it in any way connected to the earlier scene where the Ophelia in delicate white, with smeared, girlish makeup (Pascale Montpetit), enacts the 'remembrances' scene with a reasonably intact Shakespearean Hamlet? And is there any way to connect this with John Gielgud's recorded voice reciting 'to be or not to be,' with the record deliberately scratched so that the final phrase will be repeated endlessly?
>
> Critics, including this one, tend to start at this point talking about historic resonance, the deconstruction of classic texts, European history consuming itself, and heaven knows what else. But in this case it's hard, because what you really believe is that Maheu is showing off. Muller's script seems little more than the inspiration for a Carbone-14 improvisation, in the same way that a jazz pianist might borrow a bar of Beethoven and go on to create a piece that has nothing to do with Beethoven.
>
> (Conlogue 1988)

Conlogue's dissatisfaction seems to stem from his belief that a company's choices, and a director's decisions, should be firmly rooted and should all add up. A director's ideas and a company's actions are interpretative elements of staging that in a real sense come *from the text*, rather than something to be imposed on the text or set against the text or offered into some kind of competition with the text – or, that seemingly go their separate ways from the text. Of course all choices and decisions of staging will 'do' things to/with the text, but ultimately what they should be doing is 'communicating' something of the text: explaining and illustrating ideas and themes and meanings and intentions that are already there. When all is added up, a production is, precisely, a product of (enlightened and enlightening) script analysis.

Interestingly, in his final swipe Conlogue reverts to vocabulary that seems to contradict his assessment of what Maheu was up to:

> It would be a shame if this had been done to a disciplined theatre script, but in Muller's case one tends to feel little sympathy. After all, it is Muller who encouraged the rumour that he chose the title *Hamlet-Machine* because it has the same initials as his name. A writer like that deserves an interpreter like Maheu.
>
> (Conlogue 1988)

So not only is the physical discipline of the performers/performance not communicating anything of the text, it is wasted anyway on undisciplined writing. Still, Conlogue calls Maheu an interpreter, which is what he thinks directors are and speaks to what he thinks they should do, even though he has been arguing that Maheu *wasn't* interpreting so much as going off doing his own things, seemingly unconnected to each other or to the script, and seemingly unconcerned with an audience's ability to 'get' it all in a meaningful, coherent way. Perhaps there is just something essentially contradictory in the closely held belief that a good theatre director is a disciplined textual interpreter while a bad theatre director is just too, well, theatrical. But this was, is, and remains a standard line of argument. I found Michael Billington saying something similar in his 2014 review of Russian theatre company SounDrama's *The War* at the Edinburgh Festival as he 'wonder[ed] what would happen if [director Vladimir] Pankov's formidable theatrical talents were put to the service of a great text' (Billington 2014). Productions, and directors, serve texts.

I dug out my old Conlogue clipping again when I read Prescott and Cowie on *Troilus and Cressida*. One of the things Prescott found deeply problematic about the production was something he learned in a post-show talk-back: 'The original invitation to collaborate on the play arrived when The Wooster

Group was already experimenting with the Upper-Midwestern accent, so their interest in the sound preceded their interest in the play' (Prescott 2012). This revelation meant that some of the choices The Wooster Group 'made' for this *production* came before they knew they were working on this *play*. For Prescott, this just went along with his 'strong suspicion that the central interpretive choice of this production was haphazard [and] whimsical' (Prescott 2012). This is all true, if perhaps dependent on a theatrical flow chart that goes text–interpretation–production. This is very different from working with what's in the room when everybody (not just Shakespeare) has their own intentions, brings with them their own (equally) important things, and isn't in the business of textual interpretation.

Directing, whether perceived as transparent, transformative or transgressive, whether mundane, busy, tasteful or quite-possibly-insane, will always engage with the questions of authorship and intention in the theatre. A director's and a company's rehearsal process can offer strikingly variant answers to those questions – from positioning the director as the (highly disciplined) explainer-in-chief of pre-existing and somehow independent literary meaning that then gets transcribed ('interpreted') into performance, to the ways in which a group of practitioners can go about devising and determining the immediate and available narrative of any text, in terms of what they are most interested in rather than what the play is 'about'. In the case of the latter, Conlogue exactly identifies the issue even if he doesn't particularly like it: rehearsals are improvisations, and productions are the inspired result of improvising a script in its new, immediate, available contexts.

Whether or not it's seen as a spectacularly embarrassing collision, is it accurate or useful to call the RSC/Wooster *Troilus and Cressida* a collaboration? What is collaborative about having two opposing aesthetic camps talking past each other in some dialectical meta-conversation on theatre-making that only the audience could resolve – if we cared enough or were at all interested in or intrigued by what we were watching (a big 'if' for many)? Interpreting vs devising: was the RSC doing a version of the play – highly conceptual, highly directed, full of strong choices, but nonetheless a version of *Troilus and Cressida* – while The Wooster Group was doing ... something else? They were both 'doing' the text in that the lines were there, but the Woosters were doing the text while they were also doing a lot of other things and those other things seemed to be just as important if not always directly/understandably/clearly related to ('communicating') the text. It would be one thing to watch a production of *Troilus* or of *Hamlet* by the RSC and watch a production of the same play by The Wooster Group and then consider each company's approach, their strengths and weaknesses, along with one's own personal preferences. But the brilliant/infuriating thing was that both were on display in the same production, exhilaratingly or hopelessly juxtaposed. Two trains running: the real question is, which track are we standing on?

**Text and Performance: Again, Still, Whatever...**: The 'why and what for' of directing is especially important in the case of Shakespeare, because it determines the kind and quality of the relationship that exists between the text and the event. This is not meant to harp on text vs performance yet again, but it is a question of the working relationship between literal and latent textual imperatives and possibilities, and the varied acts of performance that constitute storytelling and meaning-making in this particular medium. RSC vs Woosters; Prescott vs Cowie; Conlogue vs Maheu; careful analyst vs theatrical show-off; interpreting vs devising; text vs performance ... Maybe binaries are unavoidable, and while a binary is a better tool for analysis than, say, a singular monolithic unquestioned and immoveable perspective, binaries, too, need to be pushed and pulled and stretched and remade into thinking that is a bit more three-dimensional. The stakes are not small, nor is the issue narrow and specialized. What we're talking about when we talk about directing today, and directing Shakespeare in particular, are the big questions about what stories we're telling, and how we go about telling them. And so, in the practical world of theatre-making, is the play really the thing, or is something else the thing?

Catherine Love's thoughtful *Exeunt* review for *Show 1* and *Show 2* of the Lyric Hammersmith's 2013 Secret Theatre project offers insights easily extended beyond *A Streetcar Named Desire* and *Woyzeck* (the first two secret shows) to Shakespeare and to theatre-making in general:

> My initial thought, on emerging from *Show 2*, was that this is theatre that turns the text inside out. Theatre that grabs something from deep inside the guts of a play and holds it up for an audience to see; theatre that excavates from within rather than imposing from outside. But on reflection, perhaps even to distinguish between internal and external is a misguided project which continues to implicitly judge a production based on its relationship with the text. It might be more accurate to say that this is theatre in which the text is in dialogue with the rest of the stage vocabulary, neither raising its voice nor dwindling to a whimper.
> 
> (Love 2013)

Is the director function an active one? It is hard to imagine it not being so, if one accepts that there is so much 'stage vocabulary' to a production aside from what is spelled out in the text. But is directing creative and transformative, rather than a more service-orientated or managerial position? And what is a director's and a production's responsibility to an audience? Michael Billington, in his pan of the RSC/Wooster whatever-it-was, opined that the production 'does nothing to enhance our understanding of the play' (Billington 2012). Love defended both Secret Theatre's choice to open with two very well-known plays – 'How better to challenge the structures of literalism and "serving the text" than to reimagine a pair of plays with a long lineage in this tradition?' – and the gimmick of not telling the audience in advance what incredibly famous play they were about to watch:

> [I]t allows for a viewing experience that does not immediately hold the production to the example of the text [so that] instead of measuring the show up to an imagined ideal, we are freed to watch what is actually happening on stage, in this moment, now.
> 
> (Love 2013)

Instead of presenting a director's and production's interpretation – and by interpretation that is to say something which communicates the meanings and intentions and enhances our understanding of the script, something that 'serves the text' by serving up its meanings fully cooked and ready for our consumption – Love felt the Secret Theatre 'respects its audience's ability to think and interpret' (Love 2013). There's an old acting axiom that it's not the actor's job to cry but rather to make the audience cry. In Love's (and perhaps Cowie's) understanding of how theatre works it's not the director's job to interpret but rather to give the audience something to interpret. Extending this notion a bit further, it is not the director's or the production's job to enhance our understanding of the singular text in question, but rather to ensure our engagement with any and all of the elements of theatre-making that compose this particular event.

Even so, and especially with Shakespeare, it may not so easily be possible just to move past old debates about text and performance and interpretation and authorship, even if sometimes it seems so obvious that directors and companies create pieces of theatre and so author the particular event the audience sees on the particular night. The event, and the story of the event, is made out of all the elements put into play. The text isn't the holy grail, and neither is it the adversary to be demolished, defeated and abandoned. It's one of the things in the room. It is one part of the process, not so much there to be explained but waiting to be set in motion.

**Not Meaning But Action:** What are we making? How do we make it? Here's what French filmmaker Patrice Leconte has to say about making movies:

I don't think that a filmmaker is manipulating puppets. On the contrary, I believe a filmmaker is more like a chemist. You mix elements that have nothing to do with each other and you see what will happen.
(In Ebert 2012)

Similarly, here's what musician Nick Cave has to say about another creative process, in his case making songs:

Counterpoint is the key. Putting two disparate images beside each other and seeing which way the sparks fly. Like letting a small child in the same room as, I don't know, a Mongolian psychopath or something, and just sitting back and seeing what happens. Then you send in a clown, say on a tricycle. And again you wait, and you watch. And if that doesn't do it ... You shoot the clown.
(*20,000 Days On Earth*, dir. Jane Pollard, Iain Forsyth)

Leconte is a genius, and Cave has always had a wonderful way with words, but I take their points very seriously. Directing for the theatre isn't really about interpretation, or illustration, or explanation – where both actors and audiences are the director's puppets, manipulated to convey and to consume the meanings the director has determined ('our big ideas', as Pasquesi put it earlier). For me, when a pre-existing script is involved, directing is often about working in productive counterpoint to that script, meeting it as a challenge and then introducing new challenges, tasks, provocations and obstacles, in order to create, to provoke, and to instigate action.

The script provides the plot and the incidents that make up the plot. The first time we read a script, we are not shallow if it is these aspects we are most interested in. We want to know, basically, what is happening. But there is *what is happening* and then there is *what is going on*. Actors and directors are more interested in the latter, and that is where their work is geared. What is happening is what happens – the incidents. What is going on is what gets played – the action. Similarly for an audience: there's the story, and then there's what we get out of it. What we get out of the story has something to do with the incidents it contains, and with the structuring of those incidents in the plot, but it also has a lot to do with what gets expressed through the action – the way the plot gets played. The action determines how we take those incidents on board and process the way they are plotted/structured in our experience of the event. This is *not* the same thing as spoon-feeding what a play is 'about.' It would be an odd production of *Henry V* indeed if we came away from it only thinking, 'Boy, he sure did win that war!' It would be an equally terrible night in the theatre if we came away only thinking, 'Empire sure is good!' or 'War sure is bad!' American director, teacher and writer Anne Bogart maintains that 'it is the job of the director to develop the point of view' (Bogart 2015). Point of view is neither reportage nor explanation. It is developed in action, not delivered through interpretation. For actors, what is going on, the action, is often about wants and objectives: the best contemporary way I've heard it expressed is: *'What is the character's deal?'* For directors, what is going on is about staging: the physical narrative, between characters, in time and space, in some kind of context, and expressive of some kind of point of view on the incidents even as the incidents unfold. If you like, a director asks: *'What is this play's deal?'* Again, staging isn't a particular interpretation of the action – staging is the action. A good script provokes action and necessitates its staging, but it doesn't always dictate how to do it.

Staging the action is different from choreography, although many directors are superb choreographers. It is not the same thing as basic blocking, or stage business, although all directors need to develop those traffic-direction and observation-and-replication-of-human-behaviour skills. Perhaps action is often most acutely felt in its absence. Almost all professional productions are well choreographed and competently blocked and filled with interesting stage business – that is not what explains all the unsatisfying theatre out there. The last show I walked out of at intermission was a well-reviewed production of *Julius Caesar* by a well-established professional company in a major urban centre. This production had a lot of choreography and carefully crafted stage pictures. But while there was activity, there didn't seem to be much action. For all the imagery to observe, there seemed to be no particular point of view. There was no glaring incompetence on display anywhere. It was a well-made production: well designed, well spoken, well lit, etc. But for me at least there was nothing going on – between the characters, between the lines, between the dialogue and the imagery, between the incidents and their context, or between the stage and me. Everyone's threshold for instruction and delight may be different, but I would argue that theatrical satisfaction has something to do with a production's and with our own engagement in the action.

As a director, how do I engage with what is going on in order to stage the action? One piece of staging that I'm glad I had a hand in creating was for a production of Caryl Churchill's *Far Away*. The final scene of her dystopian speculative fiction is bizarre: an extended conversation between two characters about how everything in the world – people, animals, insects, inanimate objects, geographical features, noise, gravity – everything is at war. What is happening? Two people are talking. And it certainly could be staged with two people sitting at a table talking while the audience listens to what they say. But what is going on? Since the conversation is so strange, I thought it might be useful first to the actors and later to the audience to stage one small corner of that world war. On stage were a couple of chairs and a table. There were also about 25 lamps hanging, standing, or strewn about the space on the floor. One of the characters – whose home we are supposed to be in – had a garbage bin and a box. Through the scene, light bulbs in the many lamps would suddenly go out. As conversation continued, and without making a big deal of it, the character would remove the errant bulb, place it in the sturdy, sealable garbage bin, and replace it with a new bulb from her box. This happened over and over again – same problem, same response. Eventually, as the script neared its conclusion the character could no longer keep up. The last working light bulb in the 25-odd lamps went out at the end of the show when the dialogue just seemed to come to a stop. What was happening? Two people were having a conversation. About everything being at war. What was going on? We watched a woman fight a very real battle against darkness with some light bulbs she had thought were on her side. The dialogue ended and the darkness came before we found out what else might be marshalling against her. Nothing was explained, really. But there was action. Audiences were scared, excited and charged up, and they really wanted to talk about it after the show.

In this sense, staging is not in the script, or directly implied by the script. Certainly it may be suggested by elements of the dialogue or the plot, but it comes from a director's and a company's imperative to make sure something is going on, to make sure a point of view on the incidents is expressed through action. Everyone who has been to the theatre is likely to have an example of memorable action that they would not exactly find spelled out in the script: like Karin Beier's 1993 *Romeo and Juliet* in Dusseldorf that had the 'Balcony Scene' not on a balcony but with the two lovers 15 feet in the air on trapezes, desperately, dangerously, exhilaratingly swinging about trying to get closer; like Simon Russell Beale as Ariel spitting in Prospero's face at the end of Sam Mendes' 1993 RSC production of *The Tempest*, a gesture that 'clarified' Beale's oddly neutral affect with a ferocious cap to that relationship. Sometimes the action can be more subtle. One of the most perfect pieces of staging I've ever seen I at first mistook for mere business and setting. The final scene of Robin Phillips's production of *Cymbeline* in 1986 in Stratford, Ontario was set in a makeshift field hospital: in the aftermath of war, the characters sorted out the final twists and revelations of a convoluted plot among doctors and nurses sorting the dead from the injured. At first I thought this seemed an appropriate backdrop to the action. As the scene went on I realized it *was* the action. Everyone in that scene is a member of the walking wounded, whether they are covered in bandages or not. That's *what was going on*, as Imogen and Posthumus and Iachimo and Cymbeline struggled to make sense of things. The staging didn't provide background, and it wasn't abstractly metaphorical. The walking wounded provided and developed a context and point of view for the dialogue of all these scarred survivors.

For a director, the script isn't anything like a blueprint, or a score, or a set of instructions. The script is a prompt, a provocation, and a problem – a *good* problem, and one you have to deal with. Dealing with it is how you make theatre. In its practical, creative problem-solving, directing is additive, not neutral. It is not about doing things the hard way or moving away from the text, and it's not like it's incommensurate with or somehow the opposite of Billington's 'enhancing our understanding of the play' – I think light bulbs and trapezes and spitting and field hospitals are all communicative and enhancing of their respective scripts. But directing is a theatrical rather than a textual imperative. It's more about making sure there is a 'there' there, in action, created and invested in by whomever is in the room: director, actors, audiences.

Directing: the process of making a 'there' there. This book explores some of the philosophies and methodologies around such a process. The section 'In Theory' charts perceptions of the director's job. The first chapter, 'The Play's the Thing', looks at 'doing plays' with a text-centred approach, and along with that the particular pressures and priorities of theatrical realism and straightforward representation. Realism remains the default, the weapon of choice, the looming and unavoidable template for storytelling on the stage: plays are about 'real' people doing at least recognizable things in a way that somehow reflects life as people in the audience understand it. The play can be set in Elizabethan England or on a space station in some distant future, but the basic (and basically Aristotelian) building blocks of storytelling will be the same – the creation of a world that is coherent in form, fairly literal in expression and (in significant ways) closed for the duration of the event, i.e. contained in and of itself. The second chapter, 'The Thing is the Thing', looks at other ways of telling stories and creating theatrical events – not necessarily anti-realist or post-modernist (or even completely non-Aristotelian), but ways that open things up a bit for all involved, that are not quite so text-centred or literal-minded.

The section 'In Practice' ranges over a number of productions and a variety of practitioners, most of whom are not the usual suspects of Shakespeare performance studies. I've tried to maintain the emphasis on *directing* rather than on directors, and on performance *practice* rather than performance history. While there are recurring issues that get revisited at almost every turn, each individual chapter addresses some key aspect of the situation a director will find him- or herself in when directing a production: things like the *schedule* a production is on; the *scope* of a production and the *time* and *space* it inhabits; the *company* and its particular context, aspirations and ways-of-doing; the *point of view* on the action that a production will in some way be expressing as it tells its story/stories; and, especially and unavoidably for Shakespeare in performance, the *text* and what we make of it.

# Part I
# In Theory

# 1
# The Play's the Thing

The theatre is a practical place. In rehearsals, theory manifests itself in how we address a simple but fundamental question: what are we doing here? But the rehearsal room is not a place for existential crises. It is a place for making things. So, *doing*, as in *making*: what are we making here, how are we going to make it? Are we doing the script? Are we making an event? What are rehearsals for? Are they for getting it right: this idea, this concept, this imagined production of the play materialized in its highly professionalized context? Perhaps they are for finding out what we've got: much, from many, goes into the crucible, and we give the disparate elements time to react to one another, we see what those reactions do, and we form rich and vividly theatrical moments out of our responses. *What are we doing here?* What follows in the next two chapters is a (back)story about directing – *a* story, not necessarily *the* story: theoretically and historically and practically informed but by no means exhaustive and, frankly, not the only story that could be told from the materials. The brief story I'm telling in this section is intended to set up something of the end points of a continuum that the 'In Practice' section will move within.

\* \* \*

I once received two mailers at my office in the same week for two different directing textbooks. I cannot attest to their quality or usefulness, as I don't use either for my directing class. I was and still am, however, very much taken by the information conveyed through the promotional materials I received.

## What does directing look like?

The striking cover photo of one of these textbooks shows a man in a suit clutching a sheaf of papers behind his back while firmly gesticulating to a person or persons out of the frame. Here, directing looks like a guy with a script who seems to be telling other people what to do. If there is a received idea about the role, this is surely it.

## What is directing for?

The well-dressed man with the script looks good. He looks like he should be in charge. He looks like he could *do* things. But what does he do, and why does he do it? Why do we need a director in the theatre, and what are the driving forces, ideas and theories that go with this role? One of the mailers contains an approving testimonial that praises the textbook for 'eschewing high-flown aesthetic theorizing' and instead focusing on the sensible, practical skills that hypothetical directing students are after when they (hypothetically) demand: 'Don't give me theory, tell me what to do!' In theory, this mailer suggests, directing is a craft best served, and taught, without too much theory: reason not the need, get on with the work. The photo drives this home: *I've got the script right here, let's do it!*

In his successful side industry of pithy and provocative pronouncements on the theatre (*True and False* from 1997, *Theatre* from 2010), American playwright David Mamet goes much further about theorizing versus doing. In fact, Mamet argues that the modern director is entirely a theoretical construct, and a fallacious one at that: a good play doesn't really need a director, and any argument for a director's vision is the disingenuous, desperate expression of precisely the 'high-flown aesthetic theorizing' that sceptical students and practical theatre folks should eschew (even if, or while, directing). Any theory about directing is obfuscation, an echo chamber of arty nothings meant to shore up a largely irrelevant and mostly unnecessary position. Of course, Mamet's no-nonsense polemics are themselves underpinned by a very specific theoretical standpoint, one that is deeply conservative in its writer-centred, neo-Aristotelian, plot-focused stance, and traditionalist in its disdain towards directors who think they know better than their texts and thus feel compelled to do 'interesting' things to them.

Both of the promotional mailers for practical directing textbooks are in this same theoretical camp. For these textbooks, *play analysis* is a crucial aspect of directing. Play analysis is conducted according to Aristotle's six components of drama (plot, character, thought, diction, music, spectacle) and with an eye to traditional structural concerns (beginning, middle and end, interpersonal conflict, rising action). Play analysis is at the core of things and learning how to do it properly is crucial because the director's contribution and entire *raison d'être* lies in, as one mailer suggests, 'creative script interpretation'. Since these are textbooks (as opposed to opinion pieces, like Mamet) there is an assumption that 'creative script interpretation' is a skill, and it can to some extent be taught, which means there is a particular way of doing it which is itself based on particular ideas about plays and about the theatre. Interpretation should not be the doing of interesting things *to* texts, but is the desired outcome of the careful analysis of what is *in* the text. Play analysis is textual analysis. The director doesn't really make anything, but he or she can make him- or herself *useful* (thereby satisfying both hungry hypothetical directing students and cranky American playwrights) by having a good understanding of what the playwright has made. The director may be in charge of rehearsals, the director may be that well-dressed man telling other people what to do, the director may seem to have the power, but the authority lies elsewhere: the well-trained (and well-behaved) director may be the (literal and metaphorical) carrier of the script, but the play's the thing.

The play's the thing. When Hamlet utters this famous line in Act II Scene ii he's not crystal clear about how he defines his terms. 'The play's the thing' – but is he talking about the script or the production? When Hamlet talks about 'guilty creatures sitting at a play' it would seem he means the production, i.e. the staged performance before which an audience seats itself, and so the staging and not (just) the text. So too with his line about 'we'll hear a play tomorrow' – spoken aloud, in performance. But on the night Hamlet doesn't seem that interested in the performance. He has a lot of last-minute advice for these players who are already supposed to be good at what they do, and when it's show time he never exactly shuts up and lets them perform – so much for sitting and listening. Perhaps his focus is not on the players or the playing but mostly on those dozen or 16 lines he has added to their play, i.e. to their *script* and just for this particular performance. The lines are the thing (whichever ones they are). The production is just the necessary delivery device of those crucial lines. The players are a convenience. The new words in Hamlet's customization of the text are the thing that will catch the conscience of the king.

Left to their own devices, my theatre students don't talk about the *script* or the *production*. They talk about the *play*, by which they mean either or both – they read the play, they go to the play, they watch a video of the play. This is, I think, a most informative elision. I can teach aspects of performance studies but in rural Pennsylvania often the best we can do is to read scripts. From these scripts their imagined production is something that has the dialogue spoken and stage directions followed and that's the play. If I show video of one particular production, they tend to process it as how the thing is done, and that's the play (I can provide context for the stage/television/film production I'm using and argue for distinctions in the different media/mediation, but in the moment they respond to one thing, and they call that one thing the play). It is not that they don't understand what actors do, or what directors do, or what designers do, or what different material contexts and different times and different places do – but all those things are (about) *doing the play*. 'The play' is the prime mover and prime motivator, and so what the playwright wrote and what other people do with it are easily elided. When we start with a script and its story and characters and structure, everyone else's contributions are like lenses to help focus (on) the thing but those lenses register as essentially transparent: directors direct the play, designers design the play, actors act the play, etc. – and we (wherever, however) are the audience for the play. The play is the thing, and it is all one thing: dramatically complete in itself and (not created but) realized in performance. The only thing that could make this elision more obvious and attractive and confounding is if our dominant mode of *doing plays* strongly implied its own kind of transparency.

We see the rise of the modern director – the figure, not the function – occurring around the same time as the advent of realism and naturalism in the modern theatre. And two things about that historic moment and those related movements have had long-reaching implications that remain in place today, even if they were not necessarily part of the original intent. First is an illusion of transparency of our window onto the real world. Even though most of us today probably understand just how ridiculously constructed our 'reality' television programming actually is, we still process it, understand it, relate to it and, in spite of ourselves, still believe it to be 'real' – like audiences at the beginning of the modern theatre, we are observers of human behaviour, in the controlled environment of the *Real World* house or in the laboratory of the *Chopped* kitchen or under the bell jar of the *Project Runway* and *RuPaul's Drag Race* workroom. Even though the first thing I tell my theatre students when we get to the modern theatre is that realism is a style, a theory, an 'ism' like all the others, it can be hard to distinguish realism from real, the absence of overt stylization from an absence of style, and a theory that eschewed the existing theories of its time (like those of classical tragedy and romanticism) from some end-of-history, totally transparent, objective, natural and factual state of no-theory-at-all.

At the same time, the revolution that realism and naturalism ushered in had something very traditional, unshaken and unchanged, at its core: the primacy of the writer. In his polemics on the theatre, French writer Émile

Zola offered up the philosophy but was looking for a genius writer to give the world a naturalistic masterpiece to seal the deal. In practice, we have come to associate and understand the rise of theatrical realism and naturalism more with now-classic plays (by Henrik Ibsen or Anton Chekhov or August Strindberg) than with the actual specifics of how those plays were staged. Innovation gets situated in writers and writing. Practitioners (companies/directors like Georg II Duke of Saxe-Meiningen and his associate Ludwig Chronegk in Germany, André Antoine and the Théâtre Libre in France, or Konstantin Stanislavski and Vladimir Nemirovich-Danchenko with the Moscow Art Theatre in Russia) may be argued to have been doing the heavy lifting, but the realist/naturalist revolution, for all its scientific experimental fervour, was both called for and processed in one significant way that was already understood: in terms of dramatic literature, to which a variety of theatrical craftspeople were in service.

The play may still be the thing, but how will the play now be approached? Realism's 'likeness to life' and naturalism's 'slice of life' are all-encompassing rallying cries and there are a lot of threads to follow, each with some specific implications that we still find ourselves (as directors, actors, designers or audiences) working our way through. Following on from Darwin and the origins of modern sociology, naturalism's interest in heredity and environment's effects on human behaviour removes Romantic or Tragic Man from a focus on fixed individual traits and amazing if essentially arbitrary and contrived feats and places him in a social and material context. On a practical level in the theatre, this new thinking would contribute to the demise of the individualistic star system and rise of the ensemble as more representative of life in society. The focus shifts from heroic individuals doing amazing things to everyday people doing the smallest of things – what makes people tick: let us see that on stage! A more detailed focus on behaviour brings an interest in psychology and motivation along with a focus on production design as an objective representation/reproduction of particular observable material contexts. Realism and naturalism take the theatre from collections of contrived and sensational incidents to more recognizable human stories, from grand and heroic gestures to more recognizable human behaviour, and from exotic locales to more recognizable domestic settings.

Human stories, human behaviour, human settings – the theories that demanded we look objectively (realism) and even clinically (naturalism) at ourselves and the things we do in some kind of actual social context required and received a translation into the multitude of practical matters of theatrical staging. After a time, the theory itself becomes naturalized in its theatrical context, and the style is what remains – repeated, refined and, perhaps, no longer driven by the fervour that was initially required to blow up what had become expected, conventional and false. What was left, once the revolutionary embers had sufficiently cooled, was a new theatrical imperative that still guides the director function today. If the stage world reflects observable, objective realities, a production can be measured quite easily against these 'realities' in the way that things look and the way that characters act and the way the plot unfolds – it all needs to look and feel right, it all needs to make sense. Ironically, the triumph of realism manifests to this day in a kind of stylistic throwback to one of the things realism was meant to supersede: we still have structurally very well-made plays in the realistic mode (Tannahill 2015, 35–39). These well-made plays are then served by and through well-made productions. The much maligned, and inarguably successful, French playwright Eugène Scribe's infallible assembly line of *pieces bien fait* finds its counterpart in the new assembly line of the modern well-made professional theatre production. The new foreman on that line is the director.

Playwright Steven Dietz wrote an article for *American Theatre* (March 2007) outlining a 'modest proposal' for rethinking the role of the director in theatrical creation. To do so, he makes a distinction between 'generative' artists and 'interpretive' ones. He posits that there are 'explicit' elements of the theatre event – text, performance and design – carried out by artists who make those things – writers, actors and designers. By comparison, he argues, the director's role is 'implicit' as an interpreter and not as a creator. The professed desire of Dietz's article is an eminently useful one: to elevate and empower the explicit creators, and to rethink and even retrain directors so as to move away from the hierarchy of interpretation/interpreter over creation/creators, of the director over everyone else. With that, I certainly agree. But the implications of generative versus interpretive are a bit more complicated.

Aesthetically, the idea of the director as interpretive overseer, not the maker of things (dialogue, characters, sets, costumes) but the one who makes all the things 'go' with each other like a glorified interior decorator of the stage, often works alongside the demands of realism as a style, where 'likeness to life' is used as an argument against the jarring, the obtrusive and the strange – anything that might interfere with an audience's (perhaps too comfortable) voyeurism. The director now has a job to get things just right, from the look of the environments to the psychological acuity of relationships and character interaction to the clarity and flow of information coming from the stage (now look here, now listen extra carefully to this). Where the author was the creator of the well-made play (script), the director is now the linchpin of the well-made production. As such, it turns out that the director is 'generative' and does make something: the director makes (visual, psychological, sociological) coherence, so that everything appears to be there, and to be happening, for a reason. The director doesn't make any one thing, but makes something coherent out of all the things.

Add to this the extraordinary professionalization of the entire field through the twentieth century, and the need for some central/centralized focal point to the production work increases yet again – so many people, so many decision points, so much money involved. Historically, the role of director (not the function, but the role) developed out of stage management and producing (Shepherd 2012, 11–15; Sidiropoulou 2011, 11–13). There were people-, time- and space-management issues that needed to be addressed in very practical ways in rehearsals. At some point, it makes sense for the 'artistry and organization' (Shepherd 2012, 16) to get bundled in one figure – standing outside of but looking at all the elements in play. That figure could be a visionary genius or an arbitrary tyrant – do this, do that, because I say so – or could be someone who has a good reason for everything – that furniture for the living room, that cut for his suit, that way of shaking hands, that length of pause before replying, that thought in the back of your head. To have good reasons for all the practical and aesthetic decisions that go into making a production in the wake of realism, and to be entrusted with the keys to the well-tuned and rather expensive but surprisingly delicate machine that major companies have set up to do so, it helps if there is one person who really, *really* knows what the play is about.

## 'Well, the play is about ...'

Many a preview article or interview about an upcoming production will contain a sentence where the director – confidently – uses those words. Not 'our production is about ...' or 'we're focusing on ...' and very rarely 'we're not sure yet, we're still in rehearsal'. Instead, the play is/contains the story to be told. The director utilizes, organizes, guides and edits theatrical elements (acting, design, sound, lights, etc.) to illustrate, explore and explain, in three dimensions, the story of/in the play, in a clear, considered, coherent fashion.

The director makes this happen.

The director can see the play for what it is – that's how he or she knows where it should be set and what the scenic elements should look like and how it should be lit and costumed, and can see all those things in advance. In rehearsal, the director is the play's analyst. The director puts the play on the couch, as it were, and applies a talking cure ('table work') to get the play to yield its deepest secrets, its hopes and fears, and brings them to consciousness, to the light of day or at least the work lights of the rehearsal room, for the group of actors assembled to make something from. The director is the interpreter, working on behalf of other theatre practitioners and on behalf of the audience. 'Interpretation' could mean bringing to bear some brilliant and/or bizarre concept to tie everything together. It could also simply mean helping to translate – to interpret – what the script is saying so that actors and designers and technicians can say it in their way so that audiences can understand it clearly during its eventual two hours' traffic of the stage.

And so where does that path eventually lead, when the chief administrator and artist-in-chief are combined in a single role? In this often conservative medium, we can see those two strands working towards similarly conservative ends. As the chief administrator, the foreman on the assembly line of the well-made production, the director may serve not so much as the leader or instigator of creative risk taking in a live and therefore fundamentally unpredictable medium, but rather as a risk management specialist entrusted to make sure everything works and in a way that makes sense to the majority of audiences. To be sure, there may be new and interesting inflections here and there, but those smaller risks will be insulated in productions that are, as Jordan Tannahill dissects in his brilliant polemic *Theatre of the Unimpressed* (2015), 'well-plotted, well-acted, well-designed, well-intentioned [and] well-received ... a prevailing, predictable theatre that's risk-averse and wary of failure' (12–13): theatre not intended for shaking the audience up or for shaking the art form up.

We may also see artistic conservatism (and I simply mean that in the sense of preserving rather than changing, shoring up rather than shaking up) in the whole notion of what exactly a director interpreting a play means – it's not something a director *does* so much as something a director *finds*. Michael Grandage, former Artistic Director of the Donmar Warehouse, puts it this way:

> [A] key thing for me ... is that it's quite important to get up every morning and say 'I am an interpretive artist, not a creative artist.' Of course I believe myself to be an interpretive artist with a huge creative brief, but I am the interpretive artist in the mix while the creative artist is the writer. They are the source material; that's what we are all gathered in the room to interpret.
> 
> (Shepherd 2012, 188)

Turning specifically to Shakespeare, Grandage says that 'of crucial importance to a good interpretive artist' is a desire (and, presumably an ability) for getting back into the dead writer's head to try and understand why he wanted to say this in one scene and that in another ... then you as an interpretive artist will be able to present that clear narrative to an audience which will allow them access to the deep path of the play.

(Ibid.)

A play has a deep and clear path. Our guide and interpreter, the director, is there to help us with what it says and where it goes. To do that, the director must go somewhere other people simply can't: into the writer's head. How do you do that? How do you know when you are there? Grandage doesn't exactly say. But what he does make clear is that you look in the script (he specifically says it isn't in 'trying to understand the life of the writer') and what you eventually find there are intentions – the 'why this' and 'why that'. While creating nothing, a good director will be able to find the why and 'interpret' it into the how. It's all in the play. The play remains the thing even as the director assumes an indispensable position in relation to it.

This is not an altogether unreasonable way to make theatre, and much good theatre has doubtless been made on this directorial model. One might also see it as magical, circular thinking. I was once shown the 'script' for a production of *Measure for Measure* directed by a Very Important Personage many years ago in Toronto. The typescript was hundreds of pages long, and it contained every aspect of what was going to happen in the production, along the lines of 'Angelo walks briskly to the front of the stage, raises his left hand above his brow and pauses'. The person who showed me the script was playing a small role in the show and she later confirmed that yes, rehearsals consisted of getting together and doing exactly what the director had written into the typescript. Like Grandage on that deep path, this director had gone into the script, found all the whys, interpreted them into hows, and then transcribed everything back into the script he had gotten it from in the first place. Maybe this director liked to be well-prepared. But it was extraordinary to see, in print, the entirety of the production in the script a month before rehearsals began.

There are other implications to a philosophy of the play's the thing that come to be enacted through the entire theatrical ecosystem. It is a philosophy that influences the way plays and theatre get made, especially through current standard practices of new play development. There is a writing period, then readings, then rewrites, then more readings, then more rewrites, then maybe a staged reading or a workshop where a director and actors may spend a few days on it, then more rewriting, then more readings, etc. The successful new play, the one that finally emerges from this 'bettering' process into actual production, will then most likely get two or three weeks of rehearsals before it goes into tech and then opens. In other words, the play is expected to be 'done' before any actors/directors/designers/choreographers get their brief moments with it as *makers* rather than readers. These development hours don't lie, and they serve an ideology of the play's the thing rather than the playing. The American playwright's collective 13P, which ran in New York from 2003 to 2012, was set up precisely to deal with the frustration of these endless development stages which amounted to writing it, listening to it, writing it again, listening to it again – in other words, writing plays without time and space and actors' bodies and physical materials and all the things that make plays pieces of theatre. As one of the collective's members put it, endless readings 'train your ear more and more and more, but you lose contact with other incredibly important aspects of production' which means that then 'plays function on a narrower and narrower bandwidth' (Novek 2015). There is a certain way of doing things in this professional model that gives rise to certain kinds of plays that feed back into certain ideas of how to make theatre and a certain notion of the director's role in all this. Again, it is risk-averse because it is predicated on everything being there and being ready to work 'in the play'. As Jordan Tannahill suggests, in this particular ecology of well-made plays and their well-made productions, 'most plays and most theatre artists never have the time or space to learn from their shortcomings' (2015, 79). Playwright Samuel Beckett's line 'Fail better!' – co-opted from *Worstward Ho* (1983) as a motivational maxim by Silicon Valley, venture capitalists and Swiss tennis stars – has somehow been rewritten in the theatre precisely to avoid messy, costly, overt and tangible failure through a process where plays 'Develop better!' by getting them to 'Read better!' There are, of course, other models – what Tannahill calls 'a dark-horse theatre that's predicated on risk and failure as preconditions of a transformative live event' (2015, 13) – and the next chapter charts ways of grounding time and space and practitioners in some other theories of making.

# 2
# The Thing is the Thing

Anne Bogart can, from certain angles, look like a director in the traditional mould. She is clearly the leader of her company (the Saratoga International Theater Institute, or SITI Company) and she inspires the kind of awe in others one would imagine only an auteur or guru could. But there are two things that make her work very different from the directorial model explored in the previous chapter: Viewpoints and Composition.

Viewpoints is a set of tools for making theatre pieces, and a set of concepts that form a shared vocabulary for discussing the work being made. Viewpoints is based on the two givens in all performance situations, the two things theatre artists always work with: time and space. Viewpoints is an improvisational and ensemble-building form that encourages a heightened awareness of what is happening, and enhances freedom and spontaneity in contributing to what is happening. As Bogart and her colleague Tina Landau say in *The Viewpoints Book* (2005), 'Viewpoints is a tool for discovering action, not from psychology or backstory, but from immediate physical stimuli' (125) – in other words, the things that are occurring in time and space, now, in the room, with the people you've got and what they're actually doing. Directors and actors use Viewpoints equally. Crucially to this 'philosophy translated into a technique' (7), Viewpoints training is in many ways an antidote to the authoritarian Daddy Director model, which can often lead to the infantilization of actors to the point where they feel their job is mostly to wait for a director to tell them what to do. Working with Viewpoints (of time: Tempo,

Duration, Repetition, Kinesthetic Response; and of space: Spatial Relations, Shape, Gesture, Architecture, Topography) can mean that actors sense and see from within the things a director typically senses and sees from without.

Composition is the practice of selecting and arranging the separate components of theatrical language for the purpose of generating a bold and cohesive work of art.

> Composition is a natural extension of Viewpoints training. It is the act of writing as a group, in time and space, using the language of the theatre. Participants create short pieces for the stage by putting together raw material into a form that is repeatable, theatrical, communicative and dramatic. The process of creating Compositions is by nature collaborative: within a short amount of time, participants arrive at solutions to certain delineated tasks. These solutions, arranged and performed as a piece, are what constitutes a Composition.
> (Bogart and Landau 2005, 137)

Compositions are 'an opportunity to sketch ideas in time and space' (153) so as to explore questions, solve puzzles, fulfil tasks and make some decisions. It is event-writing: it forms the building blocks of newly devised work or leads into devising the action during rehearsals of existing scripts.

At any given moment – in Viewpoints, Composition and devising – the most important thing might be the bend of a wrist, or the particular placement of a cliplight, or how close to a wall someone gets, or a fully inhabited stillness. Among the company, at any given moment the 'one in charge' is the one who has the scent – the others follow whoever has the scent until someone else has it and the group responds to set off in new directions. Directing becomes more of a collaborative and curatorial exercise within this collective event-writing. The play is not the thing, dialogue is not the thing, psychological realism is not the thing, pre-existing intention (of the playwright, or the director, or the actors) is not the thing. The thing is the thing – whatever theatrical element points most clearly towards the action and the event, in the moment, is the thing. It is immediate and experiential: the thing is the thing, not the interpretation or explanation of some other thing. It is neither illusory nor mimetic: the thing is the thing, not a representation or imitation of some other 'real' thing. Disbelief does not have to be suspended because belief isn't really being encouraged. It is a methodology that owes a theoretical debt to both Artaud and Brecht and is exemplary of the postdramatic theatre of today.

**Total Theatre, Epic Theatre:** French actor, director and writer Antonin Artaud rejected the notion that performance was just some dim echo of textual authority, and his rallying cry of 'no more masterpieces' was in part an attempt to privilege the event over the written word. Years later, work in performance studies followed on from his insights in showing that the entire constellation of signifiers that cluster in and around a production can convey as much meaning as the dialogue of the playtext. But in his moment Artaud was up against the one thing that seemed impervious to any previous theatrical revolution: the primacy of the text and, in the realistic theatre, the consistent and seamless totality of its manifestation on the stage. Artaud came out of the surrealist movement. His theories express dissatisfaction with the theatre's adherence to objective and observable realities and concomitant insistence on psychological acuity and consistency, as if people are somehow knowable and so replicable on a stage:

> Psychology, which works relentlessly to reduce the unknown to the known, to the quotidian and the ordinary, is the cause of the theater's abasement and its fearful loss of energy, which seems to me to have reached its lowest point.
>
> (Artaud 1958, 77)

His interest was not in the observable world but in the dream world, and not with conscious intention but with unconscious urges.

First and foremost, Artaud sought the disengagement of written text and theatre, where anything that could be done on stage was only in subservience to, determined by, and as illustration of the written wor(l)d:

> So long as the *Mise en Scene* remains, even in the minds of the boldest directors, a simple means of presentation, an accessory mode of expressing the work, a sort of spectacular intermediary with no significance of its own, it will be valuable only to the degree it succeeds in hiding itself behind the works it is pretending to serve. And this will continue as long as the major interest in a performed work is in its text, as long as literature takes precedence over the kind of performance improperly called spectacle, with everything pejorative, accessory, ephemeral, and external that that term carries with it.
>
> Here is what seems to me an elementary truth that must precede any other: namely, that the theater, an independent and autonomous art, must, in order to revive or simply to live, realize what differentiates it from text, pure speech, literature, and all other fixed and written means.
>
> (Artaud 1958, 105–06)

Artaud argued instead for a new language of the theatre beyond words, dialogue and character psychology:

> I say that the stage is a concrete physical place which asks to be filled, and to be given its own concrete language to speak. ... What [does] this physical language consis[t] of, this solidified, materialized language by means of which theater is able to differentiate itself from speech. It consists of everything that occupies the stage, everything that can be manifested and expressed materially on a stage and that is addressed first of all to the senses instead of being addressed primarily to the mind as is the language of words.
> 
> (Artaud 1958, 37–38)

Artaud's ideas certainly open up space for the auteur director (as opposed to the dramaturg-director) and for Director's Theatre more generally. His theories also shook up the notion of the kinds of spaces theatre might be made in, and called for a different notion of the performer–audience relationship. But most importantly, Artaud strikes at the continued happy existence of the well-made play and the director's job in that limited world of illustrating its coherence in creating the well-made production.

German writer and director Bertolt Brecht applied a materialist's concern with the constructedness of the world to both the content and the form of his theatre. For Brecht, the 'realistic' and the 'natural' implied inevitability in human lives and the impossibility of change: the visual grammar of 'likeness to life' bleeds into a kind of moral/social inertia of 'life is like that' – curtain down, end of story. Brecht thought it was a political and theatrical imperative to reveal the 'natural' and 'life-like' as socially constructed. Going against the so-common-as-to-be-invisible Aristotelian construction of drama that survived through the realist revolution mostly unscathed, Brecht did not accept or utilize straightforward action of direct cause and single effect – he wanted a number of options and hence responses to result from any given circumstances. In a rejection of psycho-realist acting, Brecht felt there was no such thing as a unified or consistent character. He felt that human behaviour is constructed, in different ways by different social relations. 'Character' is neither some essential attribute nor a collection of discernable and understandable intentions but only exists in a context. His plays explore social relations and contexts, not set psychology and internally consistent motivation.

Brecht's theatre is most associated with something badly translated and even more poorly understood as the Alienation Effect – *Verfremdungseffekt*. Brecht did not want the audience to get swept along by the performer or the playworld as comfortable voyeurs gazing upon a laboratory 'experiment' that had actually all been worked out for them in advance. The realistic theatre of unity, seamlessness, illusions of reality ... Brecht wanted none of those things. His Epic Theatre of fragmentary scenes and overt theatricality (in its anti-seamlessness of each element for itself) was meant to alternate between engaging the audience through empathetic responses to characters and situations *and* allowing them distance to evaluate or re-evaluate those responses – not strictly anti-emotional, but asking the audience to consider what issues give rise to these emotions, so that we are not let off the hook in terms of what the play raises by a mere release of feeling. Watching a traditional realistic play, we may say to ourselves, 'Life is like that' and then nod our heads or dry our tears, get into our cars and go home. Brecht wanted us to watch the play and say: 'Stop. How did we get here? Life does not have to be like that – there must be other options.' Those options are *not in the play*. They can only be found, explored and implemented in the spectators' actual lives, as opposed to offered up and contained within the totality of a textual world and the stage world a director and production traditionally supply to illustrate it. For Brecht, neither the writer nor the director can be the final authority. Whatever the play 'means' has to be worked out with us and cannot be worked out for us.

**Postdramatic Theatre:** 'Every so often you come across a book that seems to put into words a whole collection of thoughts that have been flying around your head' – so begins *Guardian* critic Andrew Haydon in a 2008 theatre blog on his newspaper's website in praise of Hans-Thies Lehmann's *Postdramatic Theatre*. Although published in German in 1999, the English translation didn't appear until 2006. Haydon wasn't late to the party then and neither are we now, since many of the key players that Lehmann wrote about in his attempt to 'develop an aesthetic logic of the new theatre' (Lehmann 2006, 18) were the same ones Haydon was seeing and taken by, and many (Forced Entertainment, Gob Squad, The Wooster Group) are still very much at work and finally getting more academic press today. While not always the easiest of reads, Lehmann's book was intended to be 'useful' – both to correct the 'lack of categories and words to define or even describe what [this kind of theatre] is in any positive terms' but also 'to encourage ways of working in the theatre that expand our preconceptions of what theatre is or is meant to be' (19). And it is useful, in terms of pulling together a vast number of threads and articulating an entirely different philosophy that seemed to be underlying the most vital theatre Lehmann was then seeing.

Artaud had some striking theories. He didn't do a lot of work. Lehmann looked at Artaud's theatrical inheritors, who were doing a lot of work, and saw a need to (re)define theoretically these striking developments in the art form. As Lehmann's title suggests, the most important point is in the distinction between dramatic theatre and the postdramatic. The dramatic theatre, from Aristotle onwards and with the uncanny ability to 'incorporate' (Lehmann 2006, 22) every new move the theatre made including modern realism and beyond, is a 'theatre of dramas' based on mimesis and the imitation of an action through the plot. It 'is subordinated to the primacy of the text' – in its 'comprehensible narrative and/or mental *totality*' the text is 'determining' – and 'staging largely consist[s] of the declamation and illustration of written drama' (21). It presupposes an idea of 'wholeness' in that the illusion onstage represents a 'world' and the wholeness or totality of that world in the theatre is a '*model* of the real' (22). Even the revolutionary shifts of realism and naturalism 'continued to serve the – now modernized – representation of textual worlds' (22). The dramatic theatre is a place where the play's the thing, and where theatre practitioners provide the tangible illustration of the whole and complete world that the written play determines 'for the imagination and empathy of the spectator to follow and complete' (22). Lehmann notes that even Brecht's 'revolutionary' theories of the stage held on to a traditional form of a '*theatre of stories*' (33) – postdramatic is also post-Brechtian, in that 'it situates itself in a space opened up by the Brechtian inquiries into the presence and consciousness of the process of representation within the represented' but moves past the 'highly traditionalist thesis [of] the fable (story)' (33).

What, then, is postdramatic theatre? Lehmann states that 'Dramatic theatre ends when these elements [the determining text, and wholeness, illusion and world representation] are no longer the regulating principle but merely one possible variant of theatrical art' (22) – not gone, or completely rejected, or destroyed, just not in charge. But the new aesthetic logic is not just for improvisation and happenings:

> By alluding to the literary genre of the drama, the title 'Postdramatic Theatre' signals the continuing association and exchange between theatre and text. Nevertheless, the discourse of *theatre* is at the centre of this book and the text therefore is considered only as one element, one layer, or as a 'material' of the scenic creation, not as its master. (17)

The philosophies and methodologies of companies who make mostly devised work are not lost on textual giants like Shakespeare. In fact, the aesthetic logic Lehmann pursues here is eminently useful as a corrective to the myth of the Fully Expressive Writer, to whose intentions actors and directors and audiences (convince themselves that they) are beholden.

In filmmaking, there's a (usually pejorative) term, 'mickey mousing'. Basically, this is when a film score illustrates, or exactly mirrors, the visual action. The music matches, goes with, the visuals in an exact, one-to-one, on-the-nose kind of way. The music 'means' what the visuals mean. It's there but it doesn't really exist in its own right beyond its function to illustrate or copy something else. For Lehmann, a key aspect of the new theatre (and this comes up again and again in the other books I'm looking at in this section) is a perceptible shift of focus onto 'the authentic presence of individual performers, who appear not as mere carriers of an intention external to them – whether this derives from the text or the director'; these performers are not cogs in or necessary delivery devices of the totality and wholeness of textual worlds, but seem to be acting out something of the personal logic of their own impulses, tasks, gestures, etc. (32). The implication of presence not under the complete control of the dramatic narrative is critical to a very different idea of directing: 'It is true more of the classical director that he lets the players speak "his" discourse, or rather that of the author, whom he takes under his care, and thus communicates with the audience.' Following Artaud in its decentring of the text and a certain kind of director who functions as its (and the author's) proxy/protector, 'the postdramatic theatre ... wants the stage to be a beginning and a point of departure, not a site of transcription/copying' (Lehmann 2006, 32). The stage is a place of 'the eventful present' where 'the particular semiotics of bodies, the gestures and movements of the performers, the compositional and formal structure of language as a soundscape, the qualities of the visual beyond representation, the musical and rhythmic process with its own time' do not simply function in the background of the dramatic action but can themselves be 'the point' of the work (35). Allowing these 'present affects' (37) to function in significant ways *as themselves* disconnects the director's job from marshalling theatrical elements to illustrate the text's meanings and to represent/imitate some other thing (intended by the author, determined by the comprehensible narrative of the textual world) – it means, in a way, the end of theatrical mickey mousing. Instead, directors and productions are freer to colour outside the lines of the Aristotelian logical-dramatic structure (see 41). Elements that used to be 'glued together' can now function autonomously, and 'new representational chances come about through the autonomization of the individual layers' (51). Each individual element can and might well be the thing.

The notion that the thing is the thing does not make 'the play' into nothing, or the director into everything. Lehmann points out that the desire of the historical avant-garde to colour outside the lines initially marked

> the emergence of the 'directors' theatre' or 'theatre of direction' (*Regietheater*) as it has been called with the intention either of praise, description or defamation. ... Without wanting to disregard all justified dislike of mediocre directors in theatre, who enclose important texts into their own comparatively limited horizon, it has to be emphasized that the hue and cry about directors' arbitrariness in most cases stems from a traditional understanding of text theatre (in the nineteenth century sense) and/or the unwillingness to engage with unfamiliar theatre experiences altogether. Meanwhile, the differentiation of a theatre of directors from a theatre of the actor or the author concerns our topic only marginally: a directors' theatre (*Regietheater*) is arguably a precondition for the postdramatic disposition (even if whole collectives take on the direction), but dramatic theatre, too, is largely a directors' theatre. (51–52)

An insistence on the 'intrinsic value of theatre' does not have to signal an abandonment of texts, but for the historical avant-garde it was seen as an attempt to 'rescue' them –

> the emerging 'theatre of directors' was often precisely concerned with wrenching text away from convention ... Whoever calls for rescuing text theatre from the crimes of directing nowadays should remember this historical context. The tradition of the written text is under more threat from museum-like conventions than from radical forms of dealing with it. (52)

> The focus is no longer on the questions whether and how the theatre 'corresponds to' the text that eclipses everything else, rather the questions are whether and how the texts are suitable material for the realization of a theatrical project. (56)

Lehmann's postdramatic theatre is no longer in the service of masterpieces. At the same time, it is not exactly Total Theatre either:

> The aim is no longer the wholeness of and aesthetic theatre composition of words, meaning, sound, gesture, etc., which as a holistic construct offers itself to perception. Instead the theatre takes on a fragmentary and partial character. It renounces the long-incontestable criteria of unity and synthesis and abandons itself to the chance (and risk) of trusting individual impulses, fragments and microstructures of texts in order to become a new kind of practice. (56–57)

This would seem to throw much more responsibility to each individual practitioner in the event, as well as to open up a lot more room for audiences to negotiate and create meanings along with their experience. When Lehmann explores the notion of 'defocalization' on the stage, the implication for directing as a practice that helps audiences to focus, to know precisely where to look and when to get the information the stage picture intends for them is striking, and the simultaneous action of a 'continuous present' (63) also leaves much more for an audience to do as participants in the event. In the postdramatic theatre, the 'whole spectrum of movements and processes ... have no [direct] referent but are presented with heightened precision' – these fully embodied 'ceremonial' elements of the event mean something but are not compelled (by narrative, Aristotelian structural logic, etc.) to say exactly what (or only one specific thing). Movements, images, gestures all most certainly come from somewhere, but the 'referent' (69) isn't (in) the text or necessarily even in the show. Whatever pleasure or heightened interest they invoke is only there, in the moment. These theatrical signs and signifiers 'make sense' without necessarily being '"fixable" conceptually' (82).

Lehmann offers this vivid summation of what we are now looking at:

> [P]ostdramatic theatre is *not simply a new kind of text of staging* – and even less a new type of theatre text, but rather a type of sign usage in the theatre that turns both of these levels of theatre upside down through the structurally changed quality of the performance text: it becomes more presence than representation, more shared than communicated experience, more process than product, more manifestation than signification, more energetic impulse than information (85, original emphasis).

What Lehmann is summarizing and theorizing is the same thing American playwright Chuck Mee gestures at when he says (in personal correspondence), 'I like it when a play goes: A-B-C-a hundred and twenty-seven-a Verdi Aria-The Color Blue-and Somebody Falls in a Lake.' Mee is exactly the kind of theatre-maker Lehmann is positing: not writing to be served by established production practices, but rather writing 'in such a way that the theatre for their texts largely still remains to be invented' (Lehmann 2006, 50). As with writers like Martin Crimp and Sarah Kane, or writers who provide texts of/in devised pieces, production is a reinvention of the form of theatre itself, neither textual illustration nor 'the result of [mere] self-importance of (post)modern directors craving recognition' (50).

Simultaneity is in, synthesis is out. The director's role as decider-in-chief, the pointer-out of the connected dots the production provides, the guardian and guarantor of unified meaning, is displaced into a more exploratory function, and the audience – confronting simultaneity and sharing in pleasures without referents – are now the ones who mostly find the connections and make their own correspondences. It remains a theatre of a certain rigour, where everything (including failure, mistakes, chance) is *on purpose* just no longer *to the purpose* of illuminating/illustrating the play's thesis or the playwright's intentions or the director's interpretive glue of 'what the play is about'. The real – bodies in space doing actual things, the tangible things in front of the audience – gets on an equal footing with the fictive instead of merely serving it. It almost comes as a relief, then, that 'the new theatre confirms the not so new insight that there is never a harmonious relationship but rather a perpetual conflict between text and scene' (Lehmann 2006, 145) – what a relief to no longer feel compelled to iron out or otherwise hide this productive conflict under the convention of interpretation. Acknowledging that frees up a lot of energy to do other things.

**Contemporary Practitioner Theory:** Lehmann came up with the term 'postdramatic' to describe the work he saw some interesting theatre companies doing. I'd like to turn to two recent collections that allow a wide variety of contemporary and decidedly postdramatic practitioners to talk about (theorize) how they do the work they do. The titles of these books gesture towards a crucial shift in thinking and nomenclature. Both Harvie and Lavender's *Making Contemporary Theatre: International Rehearsal Processes* (2010) and Radosavljevic's *The Contemporary Ensemble: Interviews with Theatre-Makers* (2013) are not about writing or directing or designing or acting – they are about making. Much of traditional theory and practice is disrupted, and much more seems to be possible and up for grabs, when writers and directors and designers and actors think of themselves first and foremost as theatre-makers. That being said, I'll be mostly looking at the director function, the things still eminently recognizable as directing, within these decentred processes of theatre-making.

Harvie and Lavender lead by defining rehearsal as not the 'repetition of learned delivery but the *creation* of performance' and declaring that their focus is on '*processes of making*' rather than productions (2010, 1–2, original emphasis). They acknowledge a debt to Lehmann's influential term 'postdramatic' and, like him, they look at contemporary theatre-makers who question and upend fundamental conventions of the dramatic theatre in order to think beyond the director as visionary leader, beyond psychological realism, beyond dramatic text as the starting point, beyond traditional narrative structured around conflict, etc. Where Lehmann articulated theory from product – the shows and companies he saw – Harvie and Lavender focus on process, and mostly the process of devising. This is understood as

> a method of performance development that starts from an idea or concept rather than a play text; is from the start significantly open minded about what its end product will be; and uses improvisation – by performers, but also other creators, including writers, designers, directors and choreographers – as a key part of its process. Its composition often happens concurrently in a variety of creative areas, including live performance, mediation, and the development of props/objects, machinery, text and images. Processual refining takes place over time and in actual space, so that theatre-*making* is understood to be as plastic and time- and space-oriented as the medium of its output.
> (Harvie and Lavender 2010, 2–3, original emphasis)

Traditional roles of text and director are interrogated, practitioners beyond the playwright are seen as integral to creating performance, and the audience is seen as having a key part in the making of a production's meanings. Directors and authors are not exactly dead, but in processes where creation is 'distributed' the director function becomes more 'facilitator' (Harvie and Lavender 2010, 14) – certainly that is what is borne out of the book's first (alphabetically organized) encounter with New York company The Builder's Association, whose director Marianne Weems 'works by way of facilitation, negotiation, questioning and occasional task-setting rather than *auteur*-like diktat' (21).

Task-setting is a critical and recurring methodology. Like Lehmann's awareness of authentic presence in the highly personal logic of a performer accomplishing a task, here too performance is often about watching someone accomplish a task, whether prosaic or impossible or both. This is the offspring of Brecht's maxim that there is nothing more interesting on the stage than a man trying to get a knot out of his shoelace. Instead of watching real people disappear into characters who themselves disappear into and are determined by the comprehensible and comprehensive narrative of the textual world, we are watching performers wrestle with tasks that the structures of their pieces impose but to which they themselves appear to be – are – finding the solutions (i.e. the solutions aren't also just waiting to be 'discovered' within the totality of the textual world and narrative logic, or just handed over by the director). I will be looking at this in the second half of this book, with Thaddeus Phillips's work, Little Green Pig's *hmlt*, and Forced Entertainment's *Complete Works*.

Tasks figure prominently in the working methodology of another New York group, Elevator Repair Service. As Director John Collins puts it,

> I have to find a task for myself, something that I've come into the room to 'do' for each piece, I need something to become a student of. I think as long as there's something to give over to – a book, a historical topic, even a strong formal challenge ('do a show in the dark') – and a fresh set of rules for making it into theatre (the task part) then I'm okay.
> (Harvie and Lavender 2010, 91)

The work, then, marks a movement away from psychology and motivation to the functional aspects of the task – that's where the work gets its 'attitude' (91). In another section of the book, American director Robert Maxwell makes a similar point: for his actors, motivation is not a psychological construct but rather a way of investing in a task (Harvie and Lavender 2010, 191). For Elevator Repair Service, initially unrelated (but potentially interesting) sources are allowed to coexist, collide, live together to see what effects are produced and what is of value; 'the *activity* of rehearsal is therefore often determined by attempting different possibilities that combine and displace the usual function of an object, character or spoken text without a predetermined outcome in mind' (92). Layering and compositional choices – conjunction of elements determined by composition and pragmatic things rather than intellectually rationalized or emotionally coherent – give rise to associations and connections that are new and surprising – and often accidental. Rather than having things worked out in advance through careful analysis of the text at the centre of the to-be-created event, here much is arrived at through improvisation and accident – what the company calls a kind of 'professional amateurism' (96). These accidents are treated with precision, rendering the mistakes and the making-do into skilful, repeatable actions – the accidental into the intentional, if you like. The company's job lies in 'capturing' the accident and using it as something to build with. This is, of course, a huge shift away from more traditional ideas of directorial 'control' of the elements. Lack of control and revelatory discovery in 'mistakes' figure too in Simon McBurney's work with British company Complicite – in rehearsals the company is required 'to be boring, repetitive, quiet, ponderous and ineffective. And constantly to fail. Failing is better than being reductive and correct' (Harvie and Lavender 2010, 73).

The use of compositional rules and the avoidance of the calculated and preconceived marks the work of Tim Etchells and Forced Entertainment, perhaps England's pre-eminent experimental theatre company. The company works in a kind of ensemble model that has a more collective material-generation phase followed by a fixing phase, which is more in the director model (Harvie and Lavender 2010, 104–05). In the initial phase of testing out the compositional rules, company members often defer to the 'it' or the thing or the work, as if they are not so much wilfully making as waiting for it to happen – this is similar to improv actors TJ and Dave's notion that the piece is already going on, it has its own kind of existence that they just jump on at the beginning and then jump off at the end, and to Anne Bogart's simple maxim that something is always happening, and so 'creating' the work depends on the quality of the director's attention and whole-body listening of the company. For Forced Entertainment, they try out 'live games' (108) with whatever system or structure or rules they have on the table, then see what happens, see what they can use, and start over. Eschewing the director's role as organizer in rehearsals, the one who makes individual contributions 'go together' in the overall whole, for Forced Entertainment 'each participant's creative input is self-determined, running in parallel with, but not affected by, the other participants' individual contributions' (111) and that deliberate lack of unity is mined for the unintended but useful possibilities that might rise from it. At some point, and in perhaps a more traditional methodology, Etchells will 'clean up' or 'expand' the individual pieces, make the 'major structural decisions' and 'fix' what they have in the version of the script that is then rehearsed and performed (116–18).

Québécois director Robert Lepage similarly blurs any clear lines between auteur direction and collective creation in his RSVP Cycles as a mode of making (Harvie and Lavender 2010, 163). Each actor brings a personal starting resource for discussion and collective group exploration (168) – rehearsals are a space where individual creative input is valued rather than ironed out in the process of serving the text or following the director. There are rules, limitations, structures/obstructions in place, but roles within the creative process are fluid. Action, space and technology evolve simultaneously in the process (171) – a distinct difference from a more traditional model of production where design is predetermined before rehearsal and built before and elsewhere.

'How do you surprise the audience rather than serve them?' This is the question Belgian director Luk Perceval asks himself as he works not on new devised pieces but on well-known classic texts. In a significant way, this attitude means he is always doing new plays in the contemporary moment of production – devising the classics, if you like: 'contemporaneity isn't about whether something is old or new' (Harvie and Lavender 2010, 224). How it hits is not wholly dependent upon from whence it came. He works to collapse the distance between actor-as-person and actor-as-performer so that his performers are not playing actors but are just reacting as themselves. He doesn't serve the text but serves the performers, cutting the text to the action as it is discovered and clarified and condensed in rehearsals, often improvising alterations and then as action develops making even more textual cuts (226). His attention is to the playing, not to the script ('I throw it away before rehearsals start') so that the quality of his attention is more like devising where there isn't a script for everyone to look down at and imagine an answer within – there's no script in rehearsals for the actors either, as they all must arrive with text memorized but knowing it will be altered (227). Also similar to a devising process, he creates rules and obstructions to provoke reactions in the moment (231). They are not arbitrary – he gives reasons for the form so the actor can wholly inhabit the task rather than just follow instructions by rote (234). As Lehmann observed in works he looked at, here, too, 'being' is privileged above 'acting', i.e. acting out or acting within the director's concept of the textual world of complete meanings.

Duska Radosavljevic's 2013 book is also filled with practitioner theory. In her introduction, she lays out some of the issues of collective creation when an ensemble has a prominent leader associated with it, but with new (postdramatic) practices finds that there is room for directors within ensembles rather than as leaders/deciders/auteurs operating from without – this opens the door for strong direction without simply reflecting the power relations of directors' theatre (Radosavljevic 2013, 5, 8). She also cautions against creating a simple binary of text-based vs devised theatre – postdramatic processes can and do work very well with 'existing' texts, and it seems to me we are much better off thinking about a continuum rather than a binary as much work really falls somewhere in between. Radosavljevic also sets store in the current terms 'theatre-making' and 'theatre-maker', where individuals are involved in varieties of labour beyond specific, defined, professionalized, traditional roles (12–13) – and so again there is a strong focus on *directing* if not so much on *directors*.

Hungarian director Gábor Tompa weighs in quite sensibly about the old issue of text-based vs physical/visual theatre by asking

> what theatre is not visual? There is a kind of canonic respect for text in America – even for the new plays – which kind of withholds and inhibits a great part of the theatre experience. Because what is specific to theatre is that you are not narrating a story by the mouths of the actors, you are

telling the story by the context, the dramatic context where the text is generated by the situation. You can't say any line just because it is written; you have to investigate what leads the characters to say what they are saying – what is the dramatic situation?

(Radosavljevic 2013, 45)

In that respect, one doesn't need to be working solely on devised pieces to investigate actions that are not textually determined: 'The masterpieces of the theatre are always open structures' (46), not so much open to interpretation as open to recreation and reinvention in their new contexts.

Similarly, Russian director Yuri Botusov is also in the business of devising old plays:

Text is the starting point, of course, but at the same time I create a series of etudes and improvisations. We approach a scene from a number of different perspectives. It's experimental work. And sometimes this leads to some paradoxical solutions which are contrary to the text. For me the text is not the law, which is something the critics chide me about sometimes. But that is a common issue in the theatre – director versus text.

(Radosavljevic 2013, 57)

How does the directorial idea come about?

From the play itself, of course. But also from rehearsals – as we spend time talking about life and getting to know each other – it is very important to me to be in agreement with the actors about our interpretation of the play. But above all, it comes from the artist inside of me. (58)

I think it is interesting to see the word 'interpretation' pop up here, but Botusov makes a key clarification: 'It's probably very egotistical, but when I make a piece of theatre I am telling a story about the actor or about myself, not a story about the play' (58) – the real story isn't to be excavated from within the script but is to be created in the ways the company deals with it.

For The Wooster Group's long-term director Elizabeth LeCompte the director's job is not to come prepared with an interpretation or solid sense of what the play is about:

I don't do any preparation without the company; everything we do is with the company. I try not to even think about the project before. Once we're working then I'm always thinking about it outside and preparing, but before we go in, I do nothing.

(Radosavljevic 2013, 75)

In a sense, then, her job is completely reactive: 'I just like to direct. I like to make things happen on the stage' (76). To make things happen is to play with the theatrical elements rather than commune with the text:

> We get in a room, we're all together, and we start immediately putting the play up, listening to it moving around. Only we have the lighting people, the video people, the sound people there with us, fooling around also. That doesn't happen as a separate process, it all happens together. (77)

All together, but not in a singular pursuit:

> We come up with ideas, and some ideas might have nothing to do with the play. We allow the ideas to work towards the play – so it's kind of a joining, overlapping and stitching that goes on between the technical and the performers, me, and the play. (77)

Things do go together – but not by the director assembling them with the glue of interpretation.

LeCompte has everyone there, but she is still a director who watches whatever is being made from outside. With Russian group Derevo, the directing comes from inside. The company's leader, Anton Adassinsky, works from within the ensemble:

> I really don't direct the shows any more. I don't like it. I like to be on the stage. I know it's very difficult for the others because they need an outside eye, they need advice – I need advice too because I can't see myself – but I prefer to keep going, rely on our feelings, keep playing together and day by day we can make our show. Sitting outside makes for faster work of course, you get results more easily, but I lose myself. If I open my mouth to explain to people what's good and what's bad, I stop being an artist.
> (Radosavljevic 2013, 95)

Another company member, Elena Yarovaya, puts it this way: 'The [traditional] position of director is a kind of sacrifice of the artist – to be off the stage and to look' (95). Derevo's practice locates directing within the ensemble rather than doing away with the function.

The traditional function of the text is also radically decentred in ensemble work, to the point of blurring interpretation and adaptation altogether. British company Kneehigh's 2006 production of *Cymbeline* was famously praised for conveying not the letter but the spirit of the thing – in a production in English but with almost no lines by Shakespeare. So what exactly does that mean? Director Emma Rice answers that the spirit of the thing is at the heart of a process of building the foundations of why – why do this play? – not from analysing the script but from literally rediscovering and reinventing the story. Rice encourages a rehearsal process of 'no fear' where much is tried out and nothing is judged early on. Instinctive feelings form the agenda: everyone finds connection to the story, to what it's about and why they are doing it, and then moves on to characters and core sets of words that describe them. The company then create situations in which, still without the pre-existing lines, the characters can start meeting. As Rice says, '"What happens when Iachimo comes and meets Imogen?" And you say "You've got a bed and you've got five minutes and I'm going to put some music on"' and from these elements something like a chemical explosion occurs (Radosavljevic 2013, 101–03). As a director, her productions/adaptations are not based on getting the text and pulling it apart – Rice works from memory, cultural memory of the story and how it made her feel to create the foundation with the company, before (re)turning to the textual source – and maybe not to its language at all.

Dan Rothenberg of Philadelphia's Pig Iron – a company known for innovative devised pieces as well as wild versions of classics – is also a director not caught up so much in the scripts and Shakespeare's language. With Shakespeare, the company purposefully doesn't do specialized verse work:

> Several of us had done that, including me, and I don't believe in that. I think that's a bad idea. ... I just trust the intuition of the performers and my ear to make more of it. ... I think when people work with these verse specialists they build arias and they build a little wall around themselves. So, this person who's in the scene with me and who I'm communicating with stops interacting with me, stops listening because he or she is letting me do my aria and my verse work – but that's not the basic building block of theatre.
>
> (Radosavljevic 2013, 136)

That building block – 'groups of people doing stuff' (137) – means listening and responding are more important than textual analysis and interpretation. When making a script for the theatre 'you are generating material ... you are not crafting a perfect work' – any script is 'a platform on which you launch this other thing' called theatre, and theatre isn't 'dressed-up literature' (137).

\* \* \*

The Eugene O'Neill Theater Center's National Theater Institute offers acting training, directing training, playwriting training, music theatre training – and a new addition called the Theatermakers Intensive that 'invites actors, directors, and playwrights to spend six weeks training in a single discipline and producing new works' (nationaltheaterinstitute.org/programs/theatermakers). Philadelphia's Pig Iron have also launched their own graduate programme in theatre-making to reflect what they see as current practice in ensemble work, where theatre pieces are made the way bands make music as everyone hangs out and figures out how to create some art. This is different from traditional playwriting's equivalent in traditional music composing; at least two rock stars agree. Stewart Copeland, formerly the drummer of The Police, draws the distinction:

> Composing music for readers is all about homework. You have to get it right in the quiet in front of your score. You put it on the page, flop it out on the stands and count them in. With bands, you don't have any score – you think on your feet. It's not about homework. It's about being ready to follow the trend or lead the trend. It's much more spontaneous.
> (O'Kane 2015)

A recent reappraisal of musician and producer Brian Eno sees a similar strategy:

> The genius of Eno is in removing the idea of genius. His work is rooted in the power of collaboration within systems: instructions, rules, and self-imposed limits. His methods are a rebuke to the assumption that a project can be powered by one person's intent, or that intent is even worth worrying about.
> (Frere-Jones 2014)

For the Austin, Texas theatre collective Rude Mechs, this boils down to a beautifully simple philosophy: 'You need everybody's involvement to get to that better decision' (rudemechs.com/rude-mechs-arts-in-context-pbs-documentary).

If the text doesn't hold all the answers, and the director's job is no longer pre-production disguised as play analysis, what then? To return to director Anne Bogart, a large part of directing lies in creating an 'active culture' that (a) develops skills necessary for following or leading the trend in the moment and (b) promotes everyone's involvement in getting to that better decision:

> I wondered how, in my own work, to encourage active rather than passive culture in the audience as well as active culture in the rehearsal hall.

One of the most helpful tools for encouraging active culture in rehearsal is, for me, the Viewpoints, which requires actors to make intuitive decisions about the composition of space and time at each and every moment. Once actors have been introduced to the Viewpoints, the conventional atmosphere of the rehearsal hall transforms into an active culture. The director sets up certain parameters and then the actors begin to make choices without waiting for the director to tell them what to do.
(Bogart 2014, 107)

The text and the director may be decentred but directing of course doesn't go away:

Perhaps it is helpful to imagine that there is no such *person* as a director, no such *person* as a dramaturg, no such *person* as an actor, playwright or designer. Perhaps rather than specific people, think of these jobs as windows through which any member of the collaborative team can approach the shared effort.
(Bogart 2014, 111)

Bogart certainly *works* on things, rigorously, in advance, but she doesn't *work it all out* in advance:

I spend countless hours preparing to direct a production, studying themes, history and subjects around the play, voraciously reading and then flipping from one book to the next, meandering, making detours from the research and taking occasional naps. It is often upon waking from a nap that the disparate ideas converge into an inkling of how to approach the play. This ability to make connections demands a loosening of the power of critical thought and openness to the wide universe of stimuli rather than the tyranny of simplistic interpretation.
(Bogart 2014, 119)

There is more to making theatre than can be dreamt of in the philosophy of Play Analysis and this-means-that interpretation – more for actors and designers to do, and more for an audience to do as well. As the production's first audience, the director makes space for all the practitioners in the room to contribute to the better decision, and holds space for the eventual actual audience's 'imagination and participation' (Bogart 2014, 109) in the still-open form of the theatrical experience.

# Part II
# In Practice

# 3
# The Production Machine

For all the clamour about Director's Theatre and all the attractions of a postdramatic theatre, more often than not in the theatre today the play's still the thing. When the play's the thing, theatre tends to get made in a certain way, and when theatre gets made in that certain way it helps to ensure that the play is still the thing. Why might that be? Why are the more literary aspects of storytelling (in the dramatic mode) still the thing? In the section on theory I looked at the continuing domination of realism as one factor and a particular interpretation of 'interpretation' as another, but there are some other pressures in practice as well – and they become especially clear when we look at directing more from its administrative and managerial side.

Howard Shalwitz, Artistic Director of Woolly Mammoth in Washington DC for 30-plus years, has some strong ideas about the practical difficulties of living postdramatically:

> We've built an entire play-producing ecology in the resident theatres – supported by unspoken rules of engagement, backed up by agents, unions, contracts, schedules, and budgets – that places the entire burden for innovation at the feet of our playwrights, but asks little of directors, designers, and actors other than to try to fulfill the playwright's vision in the *same compressed rehearsal periods* we've had for years.
>
> As a result, we don't often see productions ... where innovative writing, directing, design, and acting all work together, adding layers of richness and complexity on top of each other. It takes too much time, requires too much exploration and experimentation on the part of the whole

company. Whether we don't think those extra layers are necessary or we can't afford them, the result is the same. What we see on our resident stages is mostly new <u>stories</u>, because that's what we can accomplish with the tools we've given ourselves. They may be interesting or creative or important stories, they may be beautifully designed, but how often do we see the wider range of innovation, encompassing all the elements of theatre in a *re-invention of the art form*?

(Shalwitz 2012, original emphasis)

Shalwitz is mostly talking about companies that do new plays, but those rules of engagement he speaks of apply equally to companies that regularly produce the classics – it's just (usually) how we make theatre. His insights about innovations being relegated to storytelling reinforce a particular way of seeing Shakespeare, that playwright not of an age but for all time whose stories are continually relevant – interesting, creative, important – and for which the 'best' productions are ones that serve the plays with beautiful designs and 'professional' acting and the clear narrative drive of 'good' storytelling. In that sense, with Shakespeare there's always enough *in* the plays without companies – and directors – throwing all the elements of theatre *into play*, in new and innovative ways, at the same time. In this chapter, I'll take a brief look at the 'play-producing ecology' of one of the largest Shakespeare companies in the world and explore some of its implications for directing Shakespeare.

Directors make productions. Of course, we don't do it by ourselves and we don't do it in a vacuum. I helped to run a small classical theatre company in Pittsburgh for seven years, the Unseam'd Shakespeare Company. Over that time, we occasionally tweaked our mission statement a bit – a rather stolid, earnest, not entirely inspiring piece and certainly less exciting than our best work – but it was just before I left that I thought I got our philosophy, our core belief, down to something that would make a damn good T-shirt: *To find new ways to take mad risks with old plays*. That was certainly the theory. Sure, there were always things in the way of actually living by that motto. Space, time, money – the usual things a small company bangs their collective head against. We had certainly done 'well' for ourselves over those seven years of growth. From the company's origins, funded by a yard sale, we worked very hard to build a reliable structure, a working system, a reasonably functional machine for making professional productions happen: productions with interesting sets and nice costumes and enough actors and where everyone got paid. By making the machine, we could then make some good theatre: new ways, mad risks, old plays. By then refining and expanding this machine, I had opportunities as a director to do things with the good ideas and good people around me.

But for a director, it can be a real trick to reinvent the art form for every show when you are on a reliable and oft-proven-successful production schedule – what Shalwitz calls the 'entire play-producing ecology' that successful companies have worked so very hard to build for themselves. You can take some mad risks with reimagining the story, and the actors (even within a three-to-four-week rehearsal schedule) can take some mad risks with 'characterization' but the *production*, as a *piece of theatre*, will likely look and feel a lot like other productions: preshow light and music, house to half, house out, blackout, lights up ... and things unfold in a recognizable manner, however daring the individual inflections, through to that venerable old tradition of the curtain call. My shows with Unseam'd had something like a recognizable style: bright lights, modern pre-recorded music at every scene shift but no blackouts, swift pace and swifter scene changes, some kind of held moment before the final blackout. Behind the scenes, my work was also pretty 'steady' – costume and lighting notes given to designers a few weeks before rehearsals, music chosen on my own and the soundtrack assembled a few days before tech, rehearsals organized to get to a complete run about halfway through the process, sensitive and detailed director's notes (I once got a good review specifically of my director's notes) on time for programme printing, etc. I don't think being reliable was a bad thing. Certainly the shows were 'good' based on reviews and audience response and the willingness of people to work with me again. Good is not the same as innovative. For all the mad risks I espoused, I was making new productions in some old and dependable ways – even with a small, responsive, irreverent company that I helped to run and where no one was telling me what to do.

With the production machine you build, it will be easier to make productions *in a certain way*, in the mould of that production process – more efficiently, more dependably, more 'professionally'. Long before working with Unseam'd, this was a truth I had learned the hard way. Back when I lived in Toronto I once had a great idea for a show and got some great people together to work with me on it. It was going to be a new piece, a modern three-handed version of a classic Elizabethan play. I realize now that I should have devised this new piece with the wonderful people I had to work with and then presented whatever it was we came up with. Unfortunately the only model, the only structure, the only production machine I understood as a director was suited to a script that already existed. So a theatre was booked, money was raised, preliminary designs were set and technical resources secured, posters were printed, programme ads were sold, press releases were sent out – and I found myself, by myself, utterly unable to write the script I would then direct. Perhaps I was trying to direct it as

I was writing it by getting it all into the script. Perhaps I was scared to throw very raw unformed things on to the page that we could make into something, discover, in rehearsal. Perhaps my dream of devising this amazing new piece outran the first step of understanding that devised theatre was in fact a thing … but I thought theatre went script–direction–production, and I had set the machinery for that process running. There wasn't a production. There was humiliation, lost money and lost friendships. In theory, what goes into the process will in some significant ways determine what comes out. But in practice and in equally significant ways, whatever goes in will be shaped/determined by the machinery of making – and, sometimes, might get chewed up and spat out if it doesn't fit the tolerances of the machine. Sometimes, indeed, it is the machine that determines what you will put into it. If you are so bold and/or mad as to imagine a multi-occupant solar-powered urban hang-glider, you may have trouble creating it on an auto-assembly line for making Buicks: yes, you can have different colours and, sure, you can get some different options, but what you are going to want to make there is a Buick.

The Stratford Festival in Ontario is the largest classical repertory theatre in North America. They have resources unimaginable to a small company like Unseam'd. They have time and people and a rich, rich history. They have huge audiences. They have great cultural influence. For generations of Canadian high school students and excited tourists alike, their productions of Shakespeare represent what Shakespeare is and should be. Surely the Stratford Festival doesn't just want to make Buicks.

For this book, I conducted a lengthy interview (8 August 2016) with the Festival's producer David Auster and creative planning director Jason Miller. I wanted to find out from people who *weren't* directors something about the larger context of directing Shakespeare there, and about how this particular Shakespeare production machine functions. Auster was clear at the outset that Stratford is a kind of outlier in the professional theatre world. Other mid-size to large resident or regional companies do their four or six or eight shows one after another, maybe in a main space as well as a secondary space, but in many significant ways each production is a distinct entity. At Stratford each year there are 12 or 13 shows and there comes a time in the season when they are all running at once over four theatres and sharing a group of some 100-odd actors. Auster cautioned that populating all those productions as well as building everything from scratch for them creates a different and very specific set of demands. With that in mind, I tried to find out something of the tolerances of the machine that directors would need to work within.

Miller's job is to design the underlying rep structure based on the titles he is given. This is the master plan and draft of the whole season – every other department schedule is based on Miller's season design. At the very start, the artistic director Antoni Cimolino will give titles and probable locations to Miller, plus any preliminary decisions about specific actors for specific plays. This information goes into an 'iterative process' of different versions that are discussed with the different departments at the Festival then revised and redone. During the early stages of planning titles come and go all the time – there is a first vision of 12 or 15 plays, then better ideas come along, maybe a star drops out, maybe the season starts to look too expensive to support ... Miller and Auster stressed that the first mandate is to support whatever vision is given to them by the artistic director, and so they try to tweak what they are given to make it work if at all possible. They are continually showing the artistic director revised versions of what the season in rep could look like. The draft of the season, Miller said, is a 'living, breathing document that changes constantly'.

Given so many moving parts and personnel, and so much time and money that will come to be at stake, I asked about key priorities guiding the process. According to Auster, these are plays and players:

> The process starts with reading the plays and trying to figure out where it makes the most sense for different plays to share a cast. That structure of which plays share actors and which plays simply cannot share actors ... is the basis upon which everything else gets built.

The artistic director hands over titles, and then Miller and the Festival's casting director Beth Russell sit down and figure out which plays make sense to share a cast, i.e. which ones use men of a certain age, or women, or children, etc. The artistic director (AD) may step back in and say, 'But it needs to be these two plays that share this actor I want', and so Miller and Russell will start again with plays that now *have* to share a cast and ask who *else* can they share, in that case. As Auster put it:

> There is one way of putting a certain group of plays together that requires 150 to populate it, and another way of putting a group of plays together that only requires 105 actors to populate it and at this moment we are not in a reality that allows us to have a company of 150 actors so we have to put it together in a way that allows us to have 105 actors.

Sometimes the AD will say, 'That doesn't work so let's swap out some of these plays', sometimes he'll say, 'Let's change casts.' But the first governing grid is the one that describes the cross-cast between shows.

This preliminary cross-casting is done before individual directors are involved and, it would seem, with a lot of assumptions about how any individual show should be cast. I asked what would happen if, when the director came on board, the first thing he or she said was, 'Well, I want to do *Hamlet* with a female Horatio' – could a shift of gender for a major role be easily accommodated after cross-casting shows had been set? The answer was that sometimes this could be easily accommodated within the cross-casting grid, sometimes not. Sometimes the most efficient grid will leave some actors with a two-show offer rather than the standard three-show offer, and so that would be the first place to look. Actors on the same line of cross-casting but not used for one of the three shows would be easy to plug in to that third show, and these easy alterations can be done without consultation with any of the other shows' directors. If it isn't so easy, then discussions begin as to whether something can be shifted. Miller and Russell would have to then talk to all the directors involved to approve such shifts, and that approval would depend on each director and how their show fits into the structure. As Auster says,

> We make the first draft in a vacuum. We conceive the structure before we have any sense of what the director will bring to it – but it's awkward to ask a director about [exactly how they will be] directing something before you are sure you are actually going to produce it.

Once the director is set and ideas rather than assumptions start coming their way, then

> philosophically we are eager to make sure that the productions reflect the director's vision so we tie ourselves in knots to tweak things in the structure to allow the Festival to do the show the director actually wants to do. But when push comes to shove there are some things we can do and some things we just can't.

Sometimes the solution just involves spending more money, so they will figure out if they are willing to do that, but sometimes the logistics of scheduling means that two shows have to perform at the same time and therefore can't share an actor. Auster wryly noted that, for all its resources, Stratford still has 'never really figured out how to get people to be in two places at the same time'.

Directors for the next season are usually hired over a 12-week period between March and June of the year before. The artistic director may have had discussions with them in advance of that, and any offers will be pending board approval of the season. The board usually approves the next season around the time of the opening week of the current season (usually late May). I asked, beyond casting shifts, about major directorial decisions concerning design or new technologies or anything else that changed the scope of the production coming well after this board approval of a structure/season/budget. Auster pointed to a strength in the bureaucracy of how things there have to work:

> This is an area in which the insanity of the Stratford rep sometimes can play to our advantage. We have to set a plan before we take it to the board, but inevitably our plan turns out to not actually reflect the productions that the directors want to create so the fact that we have a dozen shows hopefully gives us a little leeway to have opportunities to rob Peter to pay Paul, essentially.

If they can shift resources around to make things work, they will.

> Someone is going to come and say they want their show to be super simple ... while someone else is going to say they want video projections and puppets and acrobats and animals and you name it and it's never the ones we guessed ... but hopefully we have enough capacity over each season to have a certain number of big shows and a certain number of small shows even if we were wrong about which productions were which.

As far as when on the calendar such things are possible, 'November would probably be too late' for a major change in plan, so they do 'ask the directors the moment we hire them what they want to do with the show – which is as much for the cycle of the marketing of the season as for design deadlines'.

Does this mean that directors are hired with a 'concept' firmly attached from the outset? Again, the answer was that it depends. Some key things like two main actors swapping roles over the run will likely be there from the beginning, other things like a significant change in the set to accommodate some business discovered in rehearsals may come quite late. I asked if there was any possibility of a director and cast really figuring it all out – concepts, period, designs, etc. – in rehearsals; Auster replied, 'We need to build earlier than that.' Designs, especially for large-scale shows in the big theatres, can be due as early as the summer before when rehearsals don't start until the next February. Stratford is not a place for wholly company-created work, or for devising Shakespeare. Auster:

> The overall structure of how the Festival works in large part works because we are a classical theatre. And so there is a sense, rightly or wrongly, that the production may change substantially ... but on some level we know what *A Midsummer Night's Dream* is. Our system is less well suited to new work that can change enormously in the course of the rehearsal process. We do our damnedest to stretch to do those things and do them well and to the same standard that we do all our work, but the system is better suited to plays where we know what all the scenes are and where they take place.

As is the case with most large theatrical enterprises, concept and setting and design are all imagined – and mostly built – well before the work with actors ever begins. That may be primarily a technical pressure that comes from producing work with the expectation of extremely high production values, but from the standpoint of what exactly directing is, it means that a play is to some extent 'known' from the outset.

What does it mean to 'know' what a play is? 'Knowing' can run from that formless hunch Peter Brook (1988, 3) speaks of all the way to making most major production decisions in detail well before rehearsals ever begin. If knowing is about a director's vision, that can imply the director's ability to act as clear-sighted guide to the journey the company will embark on together, or it can mean that a company looks to the director as someone who can 'see' it all and who has it all worked out well in advance. As Auster pointed out, in the Festival's earlier days a lot of 'knowing' the play and therefore exactly how the production was going to be done came from the top:

> There have been times in the history of Stratford where more decisions were made by the artistic director, times when the AD would say 'I'd like to invite you to direct *Hamlet* and here are who the principal actors will be and here are who the designers will be; would you like to do *Hamlet* under those conditions?'

Things are a bit more flexible than that now. By and large directors can choose their design collaborators rather than be assigned them by management (the Festival relies on a small army of assistant designers on staff to help designers negotiate the rep system and figure out deadlines). And the necessity of 'knowing' how the entire play will work in advance is no longer the norm. As Auster puts it, 'More often than not, it's simply that Antoni believes that a director and a play will be a good match, an instinct that this artist and this play are well suited to each other' and so can find their way with each other at least to some degree as the process unfolds.

But here is where directing for large and small companies runs into a similar problem, if a desire to 'reinvent the art form' is anywhere on the radar rather than just 'doing the play' in some novel way within an art form that is 'known'. Directors of productions for big and small companies have issues with time – small companies *how much*, and big companies *when*. If I am directing a show for a small company that pays small stipends rather than by the hour, then I cannot in good conscience expect my set designer or lighting designer or costume designer to sit in on multiple rehearsals and engage in multiple, lengthy, open-ended meetings to evolve the art. In theory a small company has flexibility and can more easily shape the process to the needs of the specific production, but it is hard to really do that without taking advantage. It is not just 'easier' but in some ways almost a moral imperative for a director to work things out and have clear ideas ready to hand over to designers, and then to let those designers spend their precious few paid hours just doing the work that needs to be done rather than in reacting and responding to constant changes. This is a pressure to work things out in advance, to work them out on the director's time rather than on everyone else's.

Something similar happens, albeit for different reasons, with very large companies. Building huge elaborate sets or detailed period costumes for a large number of actors from scratch, and especially in a rep situation where multiple productions are running in multiple spaces at the same time, requires a huge lead-in – the Stratford Festival has four theatres but it only has one scene shop. To make this work on the calendar, decisions have to be made well in advance of any work in the rehearsal room, and so design tends to be separated out from other processes of making the show. This either means that innovation in so many of the elements of the 'mother art' of theatre can only happen independently as opposed to within simultaneous exploration, or that those elements remain 'technical' things while 'artistic' innovation is seen only in a director's work with actors on character and script interpretation. As Miller puts it, '[T]here are directors who will journey with the actors from day one to opening without imposing or making pre-decisions for the actors. I don't see how that's possible without making pre-decisions for the set and costumes.'

There is a certain understanding about filmmaking that movies are really made in post-production, that directors get what they get filming performances but that their work with editing and sound design and post-production image manipulation is what 'makes' the film. I asked Miller and Auster if there might be any truth in saying that for a huge rep company the show is really made in pre-production, in all those directorial decisions that seem to have to be made before rehearsals ever begin – things there start with casting in theory, but working with actors in practice is actually a step pretty close to the end of the process. Auster, after a long pause, answered definitively:

> No. The fact is that no matter what preparation you do or groundwork you lay you never know what is going to come out of the room when you close a director into a rehearsal hall with a company of actors.

Miller, sounding like Patrice Leconte in this book's Introduction, agreed: 'You can't predict all the chemical reactions' among constituent elements, even when a lot of decisions precede getting into that rehearsal room. Auster picked up the image: 'It never ceases to amaze me how mysterious that alchemical process [of rehearsing] is.' For his part, Auster is very aware of the danger of becoming a giant Shakespeare cookie cutter, an assembly line of large, elaborate, beautiful, solid, professional productions and no innovations:

> We know that large, established institutions have that sort of reputation, so the current philosophy is that we bend over backwards to try and prove it wrong, so that when directors come to Stratford we want them to be excited that they have the resources of this enormous theatre, not feel like their hands are tied behind their back by it. We know that in terms of size and geography it can be easy to view us as sitting apart from the rest of the theatre community and we work hard to combat that wherever we can.

\* \* \*

Shortly after I interviewed David Auster and Jason Miller, then-*New York Times* theatre critic Charles Isherwood published a lengthy paean to the pleasures of the large repertory system (Isherwood 2016), and its resident company of actors, after spending a few days watching the season Auster and Miller began planning the year before in Stratford, Ontario. Isherwood certainly seemed to have a good time. What I was especially struck by in Isherwood's article, coming so soon after talking with the folks who set the stage for his theatrical pleasures, were a series of assumptions about acting, companies and productions.

A rep company at a 'major institution' like Stratford will bring its 'deep experience' with 'the classics' into a particular performance/production ecology:

> Seeing plays in repertory sparks conversations in the mind between shows, between periods. And it's also distinctly satisfying – sometimes even astonishing – to watch an actor you've seen in, say, a Shakespeare tragedy performing a day or so later in a classic American musical.
> (Isherwood 2016)

Isherwood describes his experience primarily in terms of a company of actors, some like old friends, some as new discoveries, all displaying great range across shows rather than simply limited to achievement in any one role. Since this sounds and was so good, Isherwood asked Stratford Artistic Director Antoni Cimolino why there aren't more opportunities for audiences to get some of this joy. Cimolino told him: 'It has to do with expense and structure. If you're doing a series of plays one after another, a rep company doesn't make sense. In repertory, yes.' (Isherwood 2016) But it would seem to me also to have to do with how you make productions and with an audience's expectations about what they are watching. Here, Isherwood and Cimolino seem to be talking about the classics being done in a classical manner – and it should not be surprising that at Stratford the play's the thing, and that there is a kind of transparency to watching great actors playing great characters in great plays. There are plenty of rep companies – SITI Company, The Wooster Group, Rude Mechs, Gob Squad, Forced Entertainment, etc. – that do a series of one play after another (and sometimes return to ones in their repertory). Even the small companies I worked with had/ have a group of actors that audiences would see over and over again across a pretty significant range of 'classical' roles. But ... here we are talking about the big companies, the resident companies, the significant companies – the theatre companies that the majority of audiences might actually get to see.

Isherwood also interviews Carey Perloff, Artistic Director of the American Conservatory Theater in San Francisco, and Perloff's comments about rep are also striking:

> I have tried my entire career to find funding to support a company. Everyone wants to fund new plays without realizing that actors are an equally vital part of the ecology. [The disappearance of rep companies] could be mitigated if the American theater were interested in acting companies and if the funding community were interested in funding them. That has proved elusive.
> (In Isherwood 2016)

Despite this, there are plenty of rep companies making new plays all the time – again, SITI, Forced Entertainment, etc. And this imagined ecology of playmaking that would benefit from a rep company of actors doesn't exactly jive with the way things actually work at a large rep company like Stratford, where so many major decisions about *productions*, about how exactly the whole thing is going to work, get made before actors come to rehearsal. It's not so much the *compressed* rehearsal period that Woolly Mammoth's Shalwitz talks of, but it surely runs the risk of being something of a *detached* rehearsal period – or at least a detaching of the director's vision/creation of the physical and tangible world of the production from the director's work in acting-coaching in the rehearsal hall.

Does it matter? Huge companies like the RSC and the National and the Stratford Festival remain places where you can see extraordinary productions of Shakespeare. A directorial stroke of genius like casting Simon Russell Beale as Hamlet certainly can change everything we thought we knew about that play. But what productions of Shakespeare change everything we thought we knew about theatre? Situating the act of directing Shakespeare at the heart of a process that also reinvents the art form of theatre is rather a different goal. New ideas about old plays that then get told in tried and true and dependable and known ways – for companies big or small – would seem to push directing back towards creative interpretation of texts (towards 'better' play analysis) and perhaps away from risky and innovative theatre-making that has a script by Shakespeare somewhere in its heady mix.

# 4
# Playing with Time and Space

There are two givens in the theatre. *How* they are addressed may be infinitely varied, but that they *will* be addressed is unavoidable. We have time. And we have space. Directing a production may or may not involve dealing with crowd scenes, hydraulic lifts, stage blood, cracked actors or miniscule budgets. Directing a production will involve dealing with time and space. How long, how short? How big, how small? How fast, how slow? How close, how far?

Time and space are the only givens for the audience as well: whatever else we may ask from our audiences, we do request their physical presence (in whatever space we make available for the production) and their patience (as whatever we are doing unfolds in time). Space and time are primal elements of making performance and essential to how a director constructs the relationship between the production and its audiences. And yet, directors and productions often seem to marshal their resources to render time and space transparent, to naturalize time and space so that audiences don't have to deal with them, rendering them known, easy and comfortable, and domesticating them into a kind of irrelevance. The expectation of two hours' traffic of the stage (and one 15-minute intermission) becomes normalized as an accepted and acceptable duration. So does the tempo of traditional structuring of dramatic action: exposition, rising action, climax and denouement (or, slow, fast, faster, fastest, slow down and stop). So too with space: the size of the world is the size of the theatre. Productions, and directors, make time and space essential elements of the theatre experience again when they again make us aware of dealing with them. What happens when we have six consecutive hours of Roman tragedies to endure, or the intense focus of *Hamlet* in 45 minutes to accept and maintain? What happens when the world of *Macbeth* is spread out over five floors of a huge warehouse or up and down an entire tower block, or when the action of *Henry V* is not just constricted to a wooden O but crammed into a 4 foot by 8 foot tchotchke vendor's booth or onto the surface of a 3 foot by 3 foot table top?

The process of directing will always at least invite bold engagement with theatre's essential elements. Strong conceptual reimagining is perhaps the (textual and thematic) engagement we most associate with directors' theatre. But engaging with instead of assuming the two most powerful givens is also a directorial strong suit, should a director actually decide to play it. Moving out of the theatre and up and down city streets, in and out of crowded bars, through parking lots and into a deserted skateboard park – as was the case for *Richie* (see Chapter 5) – is a particularly strong spatial engagement. Radically reducing or expanding the time spent on a story – so that more, different and other stories begin to be told – becomes a striking temporal engagement. Unlike concepts, which one could argue are best appreciated intellectually, strong choices with time and space are *felt* in often acute ways – they will affect an audience as they *do* things to them and to the play.

**Too Much Time On My Hands:** Event Shakespeare, where directorial and company ambition – and often creative marketing – move past the mundane going-to-a-show and explode the notion of two to three hours' traffic, has become something of a ubiquitous method of temporal consciousness-raising. With linked productions, or Play Cycles, or Marathon Shakespeare, neither time nor the plays exist in wholly discrete units. Instead, we have events like the English Shakespeare Company's *Wars of the Roses* (1987–89), Edward Hall's *Rose Rage* (2001–04), Toneelgroep Amsterdam's *Kings of War* (2015–) or The Chicago Shakespeare Theater's *Tug of War* (2016–); like the RSC's *The Romans* (1972) or Toneelgroep Amsterdam's *Roman Tragedies* (2007–); even like the RSC's Complete Works Festival (2006–08) or the Globe to Globe Festival (2012).

Marketing can create the interest, some kind of narrative or thematic continuity can make it seem like a good idea, but a director will still have to make the distinctly theatrical case that the experience *needs* all the hours, and that the show you've just watched really needs the show you will have watched after it and/or before it – that in some way it is all just *one* show. The history plays, which seem the most ripe for an expansionist theatrical project, also raise the danger of diminishing returns: how much English history of violent disagreement over the Crown do we need, exactly, before we get the picture? Once duration is introduced as an essential aspect of

Playing with Time and Space  65

the experience, there had better be some choice theatrical imperatives in play: at this length (six hours or 12 hours or whatever) what exactly is the story? Where's the hook? And why won't we 'get it' (intellectually, emotionally, viscerally) until we've got all of it? The relentless flow of history is an abstract rationale at best: something else has to be on offer for desire to be increased by what it feeds on, so we are not sated by just one Richard or a single Henry.

When the English Shakespeare Company's *Wars of the Roses* was still just *The Henrys* (only encompassing *Henry IV Parts One and Two* and *Henry V* during 1986–87), Michael Bogdanov used simple but effective director's tricks to keep me in a theatre in Toronto for an entire day in the summer of 1987, and to have me feeling that I was having one experience rather than three experiences in a row. He started *Henry IV Part One* with a handy musical recap of *Richard II*: 'The Ballad of Harry Le Roy' not only provided a bit of tuneful exposition to those who might need it, but it also had the effect of expanding the time *before* the play started to include a play we hadn't seen and weren't seeing but now nonetheless had the benefit of. At the end of *Henry IV Part One*, Bogdanov used a minor textual transposition to create such a compelling theatrical cliffhanger that I can no longer imagine doing these plays any other way. He reversed the final two sequences, holding back lines 130–60 of Act V Scene iv where Falstaff claims Hotspur as his own kill and placing them after Hal's report to his father of the battle. Bogdanov is not boasting when he describes the effect of this reversal in the theatre as 'electric' (Bogdanov and Pennington 1990, 55) – 30 years later I distinctly remember Michael Pennington's incredulity, his attempt to laugh off Falstaff's claim, his suddenly vulnerable little-boy 'come on, you believe me, right dad?' gesture towards his father, and Patrick O'Connell's sharp pulling away and killing look that said that he couldn't believe he had even put a moment of faith in his fucking lying kid. It was devastating and, as Bogdanov says, it closed this play by leaving the characters and the story 'wide open' (Bogdanov and Pennington 1990, 55).

At the end of *Henry IV Part Two*, my experience of the event seemed both to expand and contract through a well-chosen piece of music. Bogdanov eliminated the epilogue and ended with the terse and knowing exchange between the Lord Chief Justice and Prince John about a little bird telling him, and us, something touching France. It is, of course, a good cliffhanger for a play that's going to take us to Agincourt, but it was Bogdanov's curtain call – that most formal of theatrical endings – that really propelled the experience forward. Here for the first time Bogdanov used a piece of contemporary music in his sound design. Status Quo's 'In the Army Now' played, very loud, and the song's chorus told me over and over and over something that I knew *Henry V*'s Chorus was just about to suggest. Blinking in the houselights, I was processing time spent and time to-be-spent and contemplating both my investment and suddenly my implication in the action. 'You're in the army now, oh, oh, you're in the army ... now', and I remember thinking, 'Oh yes I am: I'm in it now.' Seven-plus hours into a Shakespeare history boot camp like I had never experienced before, I was most definitely in it now. Though I had a splitting headache, and I needed to get some dinner, I was also already in the next play.

Fed and medicated, I then found myself at the beginning of *Henry V* faced with a casting coup that ensured my experience of the 'final' play was not discrete, linear or stable. When the lights came up, there was Falstaff. I feel like I can remember a round of applause at the sight of him. Of course it wasn't Falstaff, it was the actor who had played Falstaff now in a tuxedo and playing the Chorus. But... I never stopped seeing Falstaff. Bogdanov kept the Chorus onstage throughout the action, and so the image of Falstaff haunted everything. The visual was made more potent – both more dangerous and somehow maddeningly, intriguingly opaque – through a playing choice. John Woodvine had spent the morning and afternoon sweeping from swaggering charm to monstrous ego to pitiable vulnerability; he had the vocal range, physical commitment and comic timing to bring the house down again and again. But he played the Chorus – often seen as Henry's cheerleader-in-chief – calmly and clearly, with physical precision and charged stillness, and vocally almost uninflected. Not only was Falstaff's absence given uncanny presence, but the rejection of Falstaff seemed to be continuously playing out in this same actor's performance of cool restraint and physical/vocal self-denial. Woodvine-as-Chorus appeared to be neither harshly judging nor harbouring warmth for his old friend. There was no high irony, and no sneaking sentiment. Woodvine did, in fact, almost nothing, and that nothing was, couldn't help but be, slyly disruptive. He let the loaded context – his pointedly not-playing-Falstaff – do everything. The action moved on, as it must, but also felt strangely suspended in not-Falstaff's presence. And so here was directing and acting doing something to me so that I had the (necessary) experience not of continuity but of simultaneity, of holding all three plays together at the same time in one event.

Other durational Shakespeare events use different temporal strategies. Ivo van Hove and Toneelgroep Amsterdam's *Roman Tragedies* turned *Coriolanus*, *Julius Caesar* and *Antony and Cleopatra* into six hours of consecutive action, but those six hours also tapped into an even larger and certainly more complex temporal frame: the 24-hour news cycle and our extended, always-connected, always-on virtual lives on social media. A large video screen showed mediated live-feed close-ups of onstage action, both intensifying and doubling key encounters and displays, while other screens offered not just English text to go with the dialogue in Dutch, but also news feeds and reality TV and films. Far from the standard turn-off-your-cell-phone etiquette, live tweeting was encouraged and fed back into the event in a digital crawl, and Facebook posting was an in-hand or even on-set possibility at one of the many computer stations, should one get the urge to share some profound thought, cheeky witticism or Shakespearean selfie; but where one might be tempted to say they occurred 'instead of watching the show', for *Roman Tragedies* these real-world habits were clearly conceived to be a part of experiencing the show. You could watch the event, watch video of the event, watch yourself watching the event, and live the watching of the event online. And when you needed a drink, you could just get one at the onstage bar.

Spatially, the show played in theatres but was designed to accommodate and encourage audience mobility and voluntary levels of immersion. Unlike the conventionally designed *Henrys* – manipulating my sense of time but living out their physical lives confined to the stage – here space also was being dealt with in compelling, hardly neutral ways. Audiences were seated in the house, but were free to come and go onstage for most of the production to visit the bar, get snacks, or take up residence on-set in one of the many couches. Action, audiences, images, reactions, responses, all was experienced and dispersed, experienced and dispersed, through the theatre, across the screens, out to and back from the web, according to the particular set of rules for dealing with time and space van Hove put into play for this production. One of the new stories of the event – fostered by the directorial innovations, the careful choreography on multiple planes, the sophisticated use of technology, etc., all for the purpose of manipulating an audience's experience of time and space – was brilliantly mundane, and more recognizably domestic than High Roman. Most of the time we're really neither here nor there, cell phones in hand, aware of but mostly just glancing at all these tragedies that keep flying past us.

Often more time and more space seem to go together as directorial strategies, especially in productions that are designed to be completely immersive. The looping and lengthened time of Punchdrunk's *Sleep No More* (NYC 2011–) went with its many, many spaces and expansive and detailed *mise en scène*. The temporal and spatial dispersal – no narrative, lots of stories, no stage, lots of sets – leaves an audience to accumulate fragments, like a theatrical geocacher without a GPS and following only what piques our interest. We keep finding more, there will always be more to find; the show will start again, we can always go through it in another way. More space and more time went together in RIFT's sleepover *Macbeth* (2014) that ran from 8pm to 8am in London's Balfron Tower block. The Shakespeare part was more tightly controlled and curated than Punchdrunk's version, but the production strategy was also to leave an audience with time on its hands to deal with: the *Macbeth*-as-theatre-performance aspect of the all-nighter didn't run for the full 12 hours. Sleeping over, in the building, became its own rule of engagement, where the space and the play would haunt whatever audience members decided to do – stay up or kip out – or however they decided to process their time and their thoughts between midnight and morning. One of RIFT's directors, Joshua Nawras, argued that the 'down-time' that makes the event so long is integral to the larger point of the experience:

> *Macbeth* ... exists in this abstract time that stretches out endlessly, where it's always night-time and everyone's always awake, so that's why we felt it was fitting to invite the audience to live and sleep in that world, exist in it in real time and experience it inside out.
> (Ellis-Petersen 2014)

More time, more space. What about less space? There are plenty of examples of what has been called Chamber Shakespeare – that's what is provided at the RSC's Swan, or The Pit at the Barbican, or Stratford, Ontario's Tom Patterson Theatre, or the 99-seat theatre in Pittsburgh's South Side where I did most of my own directing of classics when I worked with the Unseam'd Shakespeare Company. Not entirely unlike immersive theatre productions, shows in these small (if traditionally theatrical) spaces also create a feeling of intimacy, of being in the action, and an awareness of one's surroundings (and of oneself in one's surroundings) that doesn't figure in mid- to large theatres. The smaller houses bring with them comparatively smaller playing areas, and here is where a director will have to deal very explicitly with space issues: ask anyone who has had to direct, or who has been in the front row for, a sword fight on a 16 foot by 16 foot stage just how acute one's perception of space becomes then. There are more than just tighter blocking and other logistical elements (like how big a cast exactly will fit) to consider. Small leads to its own particular rules of the game, and the smaller you go the more intensely those rules may be engaged – through textual cutting, casting/doubling, multipurpose design, etc. I'll be spending the rest of the chapter looking at two examples of not so much Chamber Shakespeare as perhaps micro Shakespeare, where the radical reduction of playing area and length reveals some striking directorial rules of engagement and staging results, and raises further issues regarding the scope of the production and its affect.

**I Can See For Miles:** Where to begin with Forced Entertainment's cheekily titled 'Complete Works'? Sheffield's eminent experimental theatre company was immediately messing with one of the audience givens – our presence in the space – in creating a theatrical event for some 50 attendees four times nightly for nine evenings at the Foreign Affairs Festival in Berlin (June/July 2015) but also live streamed for a much larger audience of whomever, wherever. The idea of presence in the space for this virtual configuration is tricky: because it was streaming live, we still had to 'be there' in the sense that we had to be in attendance at the allotted time, albeit at our chosen 'venue' perhaps thousands of miles away. And presence in what form? As an audience member we had to configure our space: not just in the choice of phone, tablet, laptop or desktop, and where we were with our device – home, office, bus, garden, grocery store – but where on those devices and how much room the image was given. Full screen? Some portion of the screen, so we could read the live tweeting going on as well? In a tab that may or may not always be open depending on other work we may be doing – four hours a day for nine days was something to deal with in North America where it was on in the middle of the afternoon on workdays. The stories, told by some interesting performers, were well worth listening to, but what I want to consider is why and to what effect we might watch them.

Once we decided how to configure it on our virtual desktops, what we got were 50-minute plays, narrated by a single performer, enacted with household objects on an actual tabletop. There was something delightfully, wilfully contradictory in the effect of this: a durational event with an incredibly limited scope. Certainly it was micro Shakespeare, as every play had to live its (short) life on this wooden tabletop and the strutting and fretting players were everyday objects somewhere between the size of a pebble or pea (Snug in *Midsummer*) and an old hand iron (someone in a history play, I think). One would expect a venerable company like Forced Entertainment to be doing something a bit more with all this than, say, the many *Lego Macbeth*s one can find on YouTube. The Forced Entertainment performers didn't give the impression they were just goofing around. Their narrations and object manipulation were taken seriously, and the hallmark of the playing seemed to be coolness and clarity. In fact, the events played out on the tabletop seemed like they were being viewed from some great distance – online, I was in the front row, but without the highly engaging perspective of the close-up. In a strange and (again delightfully) perverse way, this intimate encounter was like being in the back row of the balcony at the old RSC Memorial Theatre, watching the evolving floor pattern and following the eloquence of character proxemics but never actually seeing anyone's face.

The virtual aspect may seem a bit counter-intuitive for a company that has built itself on devising – a process that usually foregrounds the performers' bodies and the physicality of storytelling. Forced Entertainment didn't exactly eliminate the performing body altogether – there was the storyteller for each play, and his or her care, precision, exactness etc. informed the story they were telling. But the body/character aspect was gone, although replaced by an emphasis on the very physical elements of spatial relations and floor pattern, at least as played out by the objects on the table. And this is highly 'task-orientated' as much devising is – doing the whole story with just a few basic objects is something of the ultimate Shakespearean task.

What seems of most interest here is not exactly how they were directed because, for one thing, I'm not sure they really were directed in any conventional sense beyond the artistic director setting the rules of the game for a series of individual company members to explore within. But they most certainly showed something crucial about directing, and I would argue that every director of Shakespeare would do well to watch a few of them. In Viewpoints training, we work on one Viewpoint in detail at a time, so that an actor's awareness of the parameters of that Viewpoint is heightened to the extent that it can really get into the bones. We might then combine that Viewpoint with one or two more, maintaining the heightened awareness of one while also starting to see how well that one plays with others. On one level, the durational aspect of Forced Entertainment's 'Complete Works' became 36 hours focused on spatial relations. Etchells' notion of this being 'reluctant puppetry' in service of revealing a 'table-top schematic' (Etchells 2015a) of each play is apt. It may be fun to think that mundane household objects became eloquent in the telling of these tales (and certainly the live tweeters were in part vying with each other to point out their condiment empathy), but that may be overstating the case and overthinking the scope of the project. At the risk of sounding traditional, I think there is only so much a balsamic vinegar bottle can do with the material, however accepting of the rules and however much into the game I may be. But the main Viewpoint in play – spatial relations, character proxemics – was eminently watchable in the eloquent unfolding of narrative through careful use of space – how close, how far, inhabited by how many or how few. What we were watching were not the bottles and cans and nick-knacks, but their relationships based on movements across the rough chess board. Through what Etchells called a 'hybrid' (Etchells 2015a) of both 'condensation' (50 minutes per play) and 'dispersal or expansion' (36 hours total), we could also chart floor patterns (another Viewpoint of space) – how the action ebbed and flowed and developed within and across scenes, and how patterns established in one scene are held in our mind's eye to influence, haunt, or find echoes in the next and the next.

Was it all a purely technical exercise? Not exactly. Etchells admits that 'we somewhat dodge the Shakespearean bullet by not so much *doing* the plays as recounting them' (Etchells 2015a) and he projects an experimental theatre cheek (and chic?) by referring to the method of delivery as 'lo-fi puppetry and diagrammatic deadpan' (Etchells 2015b). I wouldn't mind having my students see these short recountings just for the striking clarity with which they deliver the basic stories. Even so, there had to be something else going on in these truncated versions to rise above the level of crudely animated SparkNotes. 'Complete Works' was, for me, about storytelling rather than about the summarizing of storytelling, albeit storytelling through different means than dialogue. The narration was a fascinating hybrid, both paraphrasing the action and commenting on it at the same time. This yielded some good lines ('Uh, I'm in a spot of financial bother …' from *Timon*) and often startling character insights (especially, I thought, in *Measure for Measure*, from 'Isabella is … she can't even cry' following her encounter with Angelo to 'The Duke has no idea why he does this thing next' in one of the prison scenes). There was point of view in the narration, and action on the tabletop, but there was a missing link between them. It was Table Top Shakespeare but in practice, as show followed show followed show, it was also Arm's Length Shakespeare. The storytelling was clear and concise and thoughtful as well as a bit clinical, a bit stand-offish. Where I said in the Introduction that theatre scripts were not the blueprints of performance, here the scripts were performed *as* blueprints, drawings, or diagrams of the narrative: animated, but not embodied.

It may be useful here to linger on the obvious. As they themselves said, Forced Entertainment's Shakespearean schematics were not really productions of the plays. The company called them 'described performances' that Etchells said functioned 'halfway between the how-to space of Internet tutorials, to-camera cookery, computer-maintenance and maker demonstrations, and the "wooden O" that Shakespeare invokes in his *Henry V* as the blank arena for the audience's collective imagination' (Etchells, 2015a). All of the encounters were of necessity a bit, well, forced: everything had to play by the rules, and so recounting the plays and outlining their mechanics can only take the action so far. So what were Forced Entertainment's Table Top Shakespeares, what were they *really*? Each 50-minute Table Top instalment of 36 different plays by Shakespeare was actually 'about' the same thing: how Forced Entertainment dealt with the rules they were playing by. In some ways every production and all directing is about how the rules are dealt with. Often, it's only the comfortable familiarity of high-production-values realism that effaces those rules – those limitations, imposed, accepted, subverted, and somehow made virtues. Then, the suspension of disbelief becomes a polite ignoring of any and all actual realities in the room (like space, and time) in favour of the easy identification with unfolding incidents and relationships. Sometimes the 'biggest' shows – budget, cast, production values, space, etc. – have the narrowest, most limited scope, and may be the most rule-bound and predictable.

**Piecing Imperfections:** *New Yorker* film critic Richard Brody has discussed the issue of scope as it relates to modern filmmaking.

> The overall issue involving movie money is what that money buys in production, [and so] it's tempting to imagine that it's a matter of scope – that ultra-low budgets restrict filmmakers to contemporary and intimate stories told on a small scale.
>
> (Brody 2015)

Brody points out that this is of course a fallacy – even for a medium that is much more closely tied to realism than theatre is, and where the received notion of more money gets you more realism gets you more 'believability' gets you more engagement is even stronger. Brody cites a number of films that to him demonstrate how 'inspired production' along with the deft combination of 'marvels of image and imagination' manage to 'open [low-budget films] to macro- and micro-worlds of cyclonic action'. Production values do not guarantee engagement and neither does realism, and small-in-means is not the same as small-in-scope. My final example in this chapter exhibits just such compelling 'cyclonic action' between micro and macro Shakespeare.

*Henry V* is a great test of how the twin sirens of realistic representation and high production values can shape staging and our perceptions – and how production scale and imaginative scope can get mistaken for each other. In Shakespeare's script we have a Chorus who tells us that what we are to see is not real. It's a performance, and one with significant limitations. We are going to have to use our imaginations if we are going to believe in it. Yet most productions of the play, once they get going, seem to subsume the Chorus, the figure who points out the non-realism, into the illusion of realistic action of character and relationship and events as they unfold – the Chorus gets naturalized as a convention, less a frame than a gateway to staging illusion. This is perhaps especially compounded in a modern dress production during a time of war such as Nick Hytner's for the National Theatre in 2003. When things look exactly like the nightly news, no frame can prevent us from reading the imagery as realistic and then settling into our identification with it.

In the Forced Entertainment 'Complete Works' version of *Henry V*, the events of history could never overtake the narrative distancing of recounted plot and household object manipulation – the rules of the event kept anything like realism at bay. There was something of the cyclonic micro/macro going on at times – the four-deep of the battle formation suggested something of depth, as did the sheer amount (comparatively) of time it took to clear all the objects following Harfleur. Mostly, though, the suggestion of something-more-to-it came from some trenchant comments on the demonstrated action in the verbal account of the narrative. The Eastcheap scene was bookended by a barb at the beginning that 'the king doesn't come to this part of London anymore' and at the end by the imagined interior monologue of Quickly as she 'dries her tears – someone has to stay here and look after business'. The always-painful sequence of Pistol pleading with Fluellen for Bardolph's – and in this case also Nym's – life got an added jolt from Pistol's new lines, 'Look at them, they're just poor working men, they're just little things!' – and suddenly the household objects made horrible sense as just the kind of insignificant, anonymous, disposable items that leaders need for a battle. But rules are rules, and the limited scope/limited engagement of Forced Entertainment's distinctly 'other' way of looking at performance – swift, serious, cool, objective – left little space (physically and imaginatively) to follow or follow up these few choice moments. The final production I'm looking at – while not much longer in run time or larger in available playing space, with the same size human cast and bearing a number of surface similarities – engaged the play and its audience in a much more complex cyclonic micro/macro fashion combining 'marvels of image and imagination' to richer and more troubling effect.

There was definitely a lot going on in *Henry 5 Live From Times Square*, a production by Philadelphia-based experimental company Lucidity Suitcase Intercontinental that toured around the US from 2004 to 2006. The cast was small, the playing space was tiny, the means were rough and scrappy ... but the scope was epic. *Henry 5 Live* recast the play as a one-man show that the main character was performing not only as tacit justification for the invasion of Iraq but also as a rallying cry for further foreign excursions in a wished-for US invasion of recalcitrant NATO 'partner', France. Like Forced Entertainment, *Henry 5 Live* used an extremely small playing space and a lot of lo-fi puppetry, but for me the triumph and the take-away of this production was in how the narrator couldn't keep the narrative under his control or at arm's length. It was engaged, but also disruptive in its engagement – unlike, say, the 2003 National Theatre version (dir. Nick Hytner) which was meant to reflect a nation back to itself, but whose measured liberal critique for its (mostly, already) liberal audience begs the question of how exactly this production did anything other than tell its audience what it already knew. On the other hand, *Henry 5 Live* – through its framing device of a reactionary Times Square vendor (played by Artistic Director Thaddeus Phillips) who puts on *Henry V* to make a point and whose heroic efforts to do so cannot help but generate theatrical delight and earn our applause and admiration – tells us much more about the seductiveness of a war play and our role in the too-easy fetishization of its props and images. It also seems to have more immediate power and potential to disturb our theatrical and political complacency, whatever our professed politics or theatre-going routine may be.

Shakespeare's play has a Chorus who deals with us directly, and who is usually thought of (and usually played) as supporting Henry's cause. *Henry 5 Live* had its own Chorus, the Times Square street vendor, although a Chorus who not only supports Henry but *plays* Henry. The vendor/Chorus/Henry/everyone else was *always* talking directly to us, and I was totally won over by his heroic efforts, not to defeat France, but just to do the show. I was enthusiastically complicit in the actor's every move, and by extension in support of Phillips's/the Chorus's/Henry's actions – something I wouldn't be in an anti-war production, where I would be being told that I know better, or in any 'straight' production of the play where my own liberal/progressive biases would keep me from being drawn in by any heroic rhetoric. The brilliant stroke in *Henry 5 Live* was that I was implicated in the action by rooting for the performer to accomplish his seemingly impossible task. I was both too close to it (in the 75-seat black box space I saw it in) and too involved in the action of gleefully piecing out its imperfections.

> A Thaddeus Phillips work has a thousand clowns popping out of amazingly tiny boxes, but it's actually just one clown, Thaddeus, with his arsenal of old-fashioned theatre tricks. ... This is rough theatre, like a kid who spent too much time in the basement creating his own toy theatre classics, but full of magic and insight that full-scale productions often miss completely.
>
> (Russell 2004)

For *Henry 5 Live*, the toy box Phillips worked out of was a small vendor's booth, covered with Iraq war tchotchkes such as T-shirts with nationalist slogans, a George Bush President and Naval Aviator 12-inch Action Figure, Iraqi most-wanted playing cards, etc. Flanking the tabletop playing surface were two video monitors, which played pre-recorded video as well as live feed broadcast from a small video camera Phillips often moved in and out of the action. Hanging above the tabletop was a projection screen that could also be lowered for shadow play. There were flashlights for moving light effects, and small clip lights on dimmers to illuminate action in front of or behind the screen. This was decidedly low-tech, rough media. Phillips operated everything, played every character, and delivered all the lines. The characterizations were swift, precise, and telling. Phillips as Henry wore dark glasses like some tin-pot dictator and enjoyed filming himself, while the French King was simply personated by a large Perrier bottle and the Dauphin by a smaller one. Phillips as Nym wore a baseball cap with the brim facing forward and drank light beer, as Bardolph he wore the same cap at an angle and drank regular beer, and as Pistol he wore the cap turned all the way around and drank from a king-size beer bottle – shift the cap and change bottles, and Phillips was able to have a three-way conversation with himself. Most important and impressive, however, were the war toys and how Phillips played with them (and by extension with us).

The siege of Harfleur began as a man playing with battery-powered plastic tanks. Phillips delivered the Act III Chorus speech as he set up toy tanks that shook and rocked as they emitted cheesy explosion sounds and tinny cries of 'reload – aim – fire!' The effect was, not surprisingly, delightfully comic. However, the tone, perspective and effect changed when the Chorus's description-and-construction of the scene gave way to the scene proper. The projection screen was dropped down in front of the tanks and they were lit from below and behind. The tanks now cast bizarre expressionistic shadows and, with the sight of their cheap plastic glory denied us, the sound effects now seemed robotic, dehumanized and disturbing – still theatrically ingenious, no longer so funny. A Barbie-sized doll house was then used to represent besieged Harfleur. Called the 'Forward Command Post', purchased from Toys R Us, and recommended for children over 5, this ready-made burned and broken doll house featured jagged holes in its roof, blown-out windows, bullet holes and crumbling walls. The house was wheeled out on a cart behind the projection screen, and with a flashlight Phillips cast looming shadows up on the screen. In time with martial music, Phillips spun the house to new positions and redirected the light source, with the result being an entire burned out city conjured up before us. When the music stopped, Phillips spoke Henry's threats through a cheap toy walkie-talkie, again to startlingly dehumanized effect. During the Governor of Harfleur's reply, Phillips guided his small video camera through the holes in the roof, blown-out windows and crumbled walls, and these images were fed directly to the monitors on either side of the projection screen. Finally the camera found an action figure prone in a corner. Phillips manipulated the toy to look as though it was gasping, and both the doll and the camera feed died after 'we are no longer defensible'.

The camp scene with Williams and company was also played out with action figures. Henry's lengthy, haranguing response to Williams' assertion that 'if the cause be not good, the king himself hath a heavy reckoning to make' was greeted in turn by the crossing and uncrossing of the soldier/ action figure's arms, a pause, and then a considered, eloquent, damning 'huh'. The battle of Agincourt was created with tiny plastic toy soldiers – completing an interesting progression in the diminution of the fighting men from the human figure of the actor to fully articulated GI Joe-size action figures, to tiny moulded plastic army men: Henry's imperial project made everyone and everything smaller. The Crispin's Day speech was replaced with the colourful paraphrase delivered by George C. Scott in the film *Patton* (1970) which played on the video monitors as Phillips set up lines of toy soldiers on a tabletop. When the projection screen dropped down and the plastic soldiers were lit from behind, the tiny toys became rows of shadowy figures in formation that seemed to stretch to infinity as a single light source panned across the 'battlefield' and set them in motion. The carefully constructed columns were later unceremoniously swept clear and dumped on to an overhead projector. As tiny bodies rained down and the pile grew deeper, individual figures became indistinct in the tangled mass, and the lists of the dead were read out as red food dye dripped through the projected shadow pile.

In each case, what started as something like the Chorus's promised 'brawl ridiculous' constructed with toys and accompanied by our delighted laughter – it's so clever! – became a complex *son et lumière* that delivered an unexpected measure of shock and awe. Unlike (for me at least) the Forced Entertainment objects, the toys really did take over the action, and spoke out the contradictions inherent in our theatrical complicity. We delighted in the ingenuity and resourcefulness of the image-making, we willingly filled in the blanks and pieced out the obvious imperfections with our kind thoughts, and then we were left to consider our exact relationship to what was represented. Phillips and his stagecraft were absolutely brilliant, but there was no doubt that the performance was about us. The fighting men are objectified in Henry's use of them for his imperialist project, personated by objects in Phillips's *mise en scène*, and objectified again in our delighted acceptance of Phillips's image-making; but the objects themselves became eloquent as the images played out, and all the plastic arms and legs and heads lost in these epic toy battles undercut our acceptance and enjoyment of their theatrical use-value. Somewhere around the same time, the Times Square vendor discovered that *Henry V* wasn't saying quite what he thought he could make it say, and with him we found that our experience of the event wasn't quite what we originally thought it might be either. It wasn't the obvious parallels with Iraq that the production was belabouring; the scope was much broader, as Phillips was playing on a deeper and more disturbing crux in our cultural life as consumers of the imagery of warfare – on the news, in our toy stores, at this show.

Phillips's version let us have our fun but, far more than would be possible in the tightly controlled atmosphere and 'completeness' of a full-scale production, it was fun of our own making and fun that we paid for – at the expense of our complacency as mere consumers of theatrical images. It positioned us, unavoidably, as co-creators of and co-conspirators in the war games. If staging the action is about ensuring engagement with the material, striving for some kind of affect as opposed to telling us what we already know, and creating an actual experience in the theatrical moment, then this production, so short in time and small in space, was the most theatrically expansive I've ever witnessed.

Mark Russell, former Executive Director of Performance Space 122 in New York, identifies a rough and ready, direct and immediate performance style operating under the radar in small spaces throughout the contemporary American theatre scene. In doing so, he seems to be both describing what Thaddeus Phillips was doing in *Henry 5 Live*, and making the case for small means/epic scope, micro/macro cyclonic action of expansive rather than expensive stagecraft:

> Performance Theatre is a sniper in the guerilla warfare of our culture – theatre done in small cells, through international connections, via information passed in dark bars. The resistance is not to any outward oppression, but to the robbery of our spiritual lives by media, work, technology, and advertising. We come to these dark rooms to escape the bombardment of modern life. We gather together to enjoy the awkward, the wrong, the uncomfortable, the not pretty, the not cynical, the rudely funny, the extreme, the simple pleasures of seeing a person on a stage in front of a small crowd – existing.
>
> (Russell 2004)

Performance theatre focuses on the act of performing and the witnessing of that act, on the construction of storytelling and the imaginative involvement and assistance of the audience in that construction. With its focus on a person on a stage existing, it's the same thing as Lehmann's postdramatic theatre. It is, perhaps, also a lot like what the Chorus asks of us in *Henry V*. It's a style, though, that most productions of that play, even ostensibly Brechtian ones, don't or can't pursue, as star turns or big-image-making or psychological realism take over. Performance theatre is more directly made with us and so more directly about us, as we are implicated co-conspirators in its effects.

When I saw Phillips's piece in 2006, three years in to the Iraq occupation, the similarity of certain aspects of *Henry V* to the run-up to that war and its subsequent conduct seemed so obvious as to be almost banal. Ultimately, though, it's not the plot points that allow *Henry V* to function as a mediator of our political culture on and through our contemporary stages. It is the method of presentation, the strategy of implicating the audience in its effects that the Chorus is so upfront about, that Phillips recognized and ran with, and that a style like Russell's performance theatre can capitalize upon with simplicity, immediacy and directness. It's a theatrical form that is indebted not to our contemporary media or postmodern aesthetics but to an engagement with (rather than explanation of) the Shakespeare text in the theatrical mix, which is not such an unlikely place to turn. Phillips himself recognized, from within the toy box and two years into the life of his show, that his (and the fictional Times Square vendor's) appropriation of the play is really just a production that both Shakespeare and audiences adapt to:

> Although *Henry 5 Live* starts with a performance concept on top, in the end the power of the play itself is what comes out, and performing two years later only solidified that point. During the first performances, I found many critics to be taken aback by the political angle of the show. There is this profound and widespread thought that if you bring politics into the theatre, you are doing propaganda and not theatre. But *Henry V* and our *Henry 5 Live* are in the end not about politics but about war and thus life and death and how the egos and decisions of leaders can lead to totally pointless destruction. Two years on I definitely feel that there is much less immediate resistance to the concept of the piece, and that the performance has settled into becoming a solid version of *Henry V*.
> (Interview, 7 June 2006)

Before we think Phillips is just another generative artist trying to disappear into Bard-worship and self-justification of the it's-all-in-the-script variety, it's worth remembering that theatre artists don't actually think they are interpreting something, or doing a version of something, or critiquing something. The only thing they can do is what they are doing, and that is the play (see Worthen 2001, 333). Since it is a war play rather than a position paper, the 'politics' aren't *delivered* but rather *provoked* somewhere in the audience's responsibility for and engagement with imagery that so troubles and delights: direction and production leave the important things for an audience to do. So close in physical proximity, so detached from traditional psychological realism, and so gleefully capitalizing on whiplashing macro- and micro-worlds of cyclonic action, the show allowed me to piece out the theatrical imperfections in its stagecraft and to pause over the much more personal imperfections of my seemingly-too-joyful willingness to do so.

# 5
# Devising Shakespeare

With its new title, *Henry 5 Live From Times Square* wasn't exactly 'By William Shakespeare'. The piece was 'Created, Designed and Performed' by Thaddeus Phillips, the company's artistic director and the auteur of the event although not actually its director: that was Tatiana Mallarino, Phillips's outside eyes, as well as his partner in the company and in real life. Things get blurred a bit in devised work, which this surely was. For his part, Shakespeare provided the majority of the lines spoken in the piece, and saying all of Shakespeare's lines and playing all of his characters while running all the tech from within the tiny tchotchke booth formed the task and the action at the core of the event. Shakespeare was even a significant element of the *mise en scène*, although I didn't realize it until I helped break down the set after the show. When I brought the production to my university in February of 2006, Phillips hadn't done the piece for a while, so most of the Shakespeare text was typed up and cut out and taped up all around the insides of the set. Although I sat only about 12 feet away, I was never aware of Phillips actually relying on any of his cheat sheets. Perhaps he never used them once he got going. But they were there, like the flashlights and cameras and Perrier bottles and toy soldiers, on hand as needed to make the show.

Is it fair to talk about devising Shakespeare? I can understand the argument that either something is a production (however bizarre) of a play by Shakespeare or it is something else. I can also understand the argument that every production, every engagement of a group of artists with these few words from a long-dead playwright, is in effect an adaptation in one way or another as a new 'performance text' gets written for the event, and so is always a new work in its own right. In this chapter I'll look at directing

Shakespeare in some instances where the text is (almost entirely) there, but the directorial and company approach is much more from the perspective of devising new work than from a standpoint of (re)interpreting old plays.

The Wooster Group/Royal Shakespeare Company 2012 production of *Troilus and Cressida* had an afterlife beyond its problematic Stratford-upon-Avon and London run. Freed in some ways from its origins as a collaboration/collision between two companies but pretending to be one production, the show in America became much more the thing it was: a devised piece, now titled *Cry, Trojans! (Troilus and Cressida)*, by The Wooster Group with 'Text By William Shakespeare'. The 'new' show played in Los Angeles in 2014 and in New York in 2015. Without their English friends, The Wooster Group continued to play the Trojan bits while adding some parts of the Greek side of the story through mask and puppet work as well as some dim distorted echoes of the RSC actors' voices (weirdly poignant and oddly hilarious) that occasionally drifted into the soundscape. That soundscape as a whole was much more developed, some new songs were added to the mix, and there was a lot more video as well, especially from Inuit filmmaker Zacharias Kunuk's *Atanarjuat: The Fast Runner* (2001). There was no 'chemistry' between Troilus and Cressida, if measuring it in psychological-realist terms. Still, the parting was pretty fiery and devastating as the soundscape thundered and the blocking mimicked Warren Beatty and Natalie Wood falling apart furiously on the video monitors in a clip from Elia Kazan's *Splendor in the Grass* (1961). But this production's pleasures (while perhaps still mostly intellectual) come (if they do) from watching a company that is wholly committing to a particular theatrical process and vocabulary – to which Shakespeare contributed some of the words. The pleasure is that everything that goes into The Wooster Group's process comes out different.

The Wooster Group is not in the business of serving the text – it develops projects rather than stages plays. Director Elizabeth LeCompte doesn't come with a vision for any particular text but rather starts at zero and works with all the company members to provide structural frames and specific tasks that actors have to inhabit – activities, games and improvisations provide the structure of the event as much if not more than the plot of whatever script might be there in the mix. Design, tech and acting develop together, and the event is made up of the accumulation of objects, signs, and tasks and the results of formal experimentation with them. The Wooster Group is also famous for recycling absent or past performances, and this strategy figured very much in their two forays into Shakespeare. Their production of *Hamlet* was less a production of 'the play' and more a response to Richard Burton's filmed stage production of the play from 1964, with the central task of replicating live-and-now the filmed live-but-then performances.

Similar past/present loops and echoes occurred with their latest sort-of-Shakespeare. The Woosters were working with and not-quite-with their RSC compatriots for the Stratford and London versions of the show – Cressida arriving in the Greek camp was a brilliantly, deliberately disconnected sequence of being in the same room but inhabiting different stage worlds. Back in the States, with *Cry Trojans*, the company both jettisoned and made much of their absent friends.

Sitting in the audience in Brooklyn, laughing whenever I thought I heard or saw some odd echo of the absent RSC actors that I remembered from the Stratford show, I wondered: was it sly poker-faced mockery? Or were they being self-effacing, by imitating actors who in the earlier incarnation were the ones who some critics thought could at least do Shakespeare right? I was of course grasping at straws in trying to ascribe that kind of intentionality. The British/RSC Shakespeare acting became another template and style to be mimicked, became just another stimulus and repurposed original like the flat vocal cadences of North Dakota or the 1950s 'redface' cowboy movie kitsch or the Inuit film or the Kazan film. Whatever goes into the process comes out different. As an audience member I may recognize some of the referents but there is no point in trying to 'get' them – they are structural more than thematic or interpretable. They are not things that mean other things. They are the things that make *this* work, in *this* moment. They are theatrical elements that company members (actors, designers, technicians) are tasked, somehow, to deal with. Dealing with the tasks provides structure to the theatrical event just as, more traditionally, the selection and arrangement of events from the story works to structure the dramatic plot of a script.

In *The Viewpoints Book*, Anne Bogart and Tina Landau lay out a simple process or 'basic building blocks' for creating devised work:

In the creation of original work, it is helpful for the process to be grounded in three basic components upon which a production can be constructed:

- The *question*
- The *anchor*
- The *structure*.

The *question* (or theme) motivates the entire process. This central driving force should be big enough, interesting enough and relevant enough to be attractive and contagious to many people. The question emerges from personal interest and then spreads like a virus to other people who come in contact with it.

The *anchor* is a person (or event) that can serve as a vehicle to get to the *question*.

The *structure* is the skeleton upon which the event hangs. It is a way to organize time, information, text and imagery (Bogart and Landau 2005, 155).

In this process 'upon which a production can be constructed', devising, to me at least, just looks a lot like directing. However, when I think about most productions of Shakespeare done in what Lehmann (2006) defines as the dramatic mode, and where the play's the thing, those building blocks start to seem basic indeed. In traditional text-centred directing, question–anchor–structure are all elided and operating in an echo chamber of imagined authorial intention, where the question is only ever 'what is this play about?', the anchor is 'the characters and events of the play' and the structure is 'the play Shakespeare wrote'. The production may be dressed up in different costumes and periods with different sets and props but its process of creation remains fixed within these self-imposed and self-referential limits – the anchor and the structure are the play and they are used to explore the question of the play. Can Bogart's elegantly simple process be used by companies and directors to create truly 'original work' – work that reinvents the art form of theatre – while also just happening to have words by Shakespeare in the mix?

Little Green Pig Theatrical Concern (the name is taken from Martin McDonagh's 2003 play *The Pillowman*) is a small company in Durham, North Carolina, that specializes in epic innovation. Since 2005 LGP has been creating an eclectic production repertoire exploring new and classic work with a focus on the art form over the script. It almost seems pointless to talk about devising vs directing, new vs classic, with this company. Productions of complete texts for Chekhov's *The Cherry Orchard* (2006) and Wilder's *Our Town* (2013), but with all-African American casts, seemed like 'new plays' just as much as their more radical rewrites of Chekhov's plays in *Three Sisters (On Ice)* (2006) or *The New Colossus* (an adaptation of *The Seagull* from 2016). All three productions of Shakespeare that they have done thus far have had new titles – *Richie* (2012), *hmlt* (2014, a version of *Hamlet*) and *Maccountant* (2016, a version of *Macbeth*) – while overwhelmingly sticking with words by William Shakespeare. I'll spend the rest of this chapter looking at *Richie*, their version of *Richard II* staged as an all-female rolling pub crawl up and down Rigsbee Avenue and Foster Street in downtown Durham in September 2012.

Actors who have worked with LGP over the years attest to the company's, and Artistic Director Jaybird O'Berski's, ability to ask interesting and strikingly contemporary questions through whatever work they are doing. Company regular Tamara Kissane identifies that quality as integral to the company's identity: 'no one else does this work – original, risky, tied into the culture. Jaybird has his finger on the pulse on a subconscious cultural level and brings that into the shows' (Interview, 7 August 2014). For the company in early 2012 the *question* was: 'What is celebrity and how do we treat it?' The *anchor* was that golden child, absolute monarch and fallen idol Richard II (and so by extension Shakespeare's *Richard II*). And the *structure* – the task, the specific logistics governing the action – was an all-female pub crawl that would range up and down busy streets, into clubs and bars, through parking lots and back alleys, and come to rest in the empty pipes and bowls of a city skatepark at night.

I asked Company Manager Dana Marks, who also played Richie, if she could say what exactly *Richie* was:

KE: So, did you think you were doing Shakespeare or a new play?

DM: I thought we were doing Shakespeare.

KE: But, like, an adaptation–

DM: Uh huh.

KE: A version–

DM: Uh huh.

KE: A concept–

DM: Uh huh.

KE: Called *Richie*.

    (silence)

DM: I thought we were doing Shakespeare in a new context, using space in a different way.

(Interview, 10 August 2014)

Actors do the show. It tends to be critics who try to conceptualize that process. Tamara Kissane, who played Haley Bolingbroke, also eschewed easy distinctions:

I thought I was doing Shakespeare in a new dress. The language was there, and that to me is what Shakespeare is, that's why it's unlike doing anything else – if the language is there then it's automatically

Shakespeare. We did a reading of Shakespeare's *Richard II* first, then we got a rehearsal script of *Richie*. I treated the rehearsal script like it was Shakespeare's script. I felt that Jay had this idea about celebrity and star power and wanted to explore it, and I don't know how much he knew from the start or how much was happy accident, but I felt that the text fleshed out the idea but also the idea fleshed out the text. They worked so nicely together that I didn't feel there was a disconnect between Shakespearean text and the concept.

(Interview, 7 August 2014)

That seamlessness extended to the show's reception: the cycle of Kings in the Henriad reflected in the cycle of Britneys and Mileys being built up and torn down in our culture was not a distortion but just made sense. For Kissane, that is exactly what directing/devising Shakespeare is meant to do:

That's how you have to do it or it won't work. I've been thinking about this idea of 'fixing' [a play in production] and about cultural accessibility. People who originally witnessed those plays had a historical framework, a cultural framework, a political framework, that helped them key in to what was happening on stage. They had a way into that world. We don't have that so we need new cultural accessibility points, and that's what Jay gave people [through the added references to texting and tweeting and blogging, the celebrity entourages, the bad-girl party scene played out, etc.] so the witnesses, the audiences, had a framework to hang the story on.

(Interview, 7 August 2014)

The setting or context or, more accurately, the task of the rolling all-female pub crawl through immediate and contemporary spaces – that is what structured the presentation and the reception of the story for the audience, rather than (only) the plot.

The new context is also what made it possible for the huge cast of women involved to take ownership of the story as they devised its new and immediate action for themselves through the task at hand. Again, this production – which from the outside may look and sound high concept and so by implication *must* have been very directed in the sense of a traditional strong directorial vision and presence leading everything and everyone – was more devised than dictated. I was initially surprised by the strong sense of ownership expressed by Kissane in her blog about the production, written just as it closed:

In the world that we created, I felt able to push the boundaries of my experience of being a woman, well, a human, really. ... I felt, more than ever before, the freedom and ability to be *simultaneously* beautiful and ugly, girlish and wise, aggressive and fierce and profane and vulnerable, sexy and powerful, muscular and lyrical, charming and dangerous and silly and funny, superficial and deep deep deep WOMAN. This is big for me. This open-source complexity is something I believe in, but have never fully owned. In the world of this play, serious gorgeous Shakespearean verse could co-exist with four-letter-words as tools wielded by women doing business and living life. It was warrior and princess, madonna and whore, a mash-up of masculine/feminine without compartmentalizing or categorizing. I don't know if this was due to the absence of male characters or the overwhelming presence of female characters (19 of us), but there was some heady female alchemy present.

So, in my mind, my character chose her costume because *she* liked it (short-shorts, tummy-showing blouse, a wig, false eyelashes, knee-high boots, a metric ton of red lipstick) and not because some dude might think it was hot. There were no dudes in the world of RICHIE. And no offense, Dudes, but it was nice to have some play-time in a land without you for a little while. It was fierce female power on-stage *(how liberating!)*. And off-stage, the women (and the few fab guys too) were generous professionals who brought their 'A games' and were all bent on telling a kick-ass story.

(tamarakissane.com/2012/09, 24 September 2012)

'Open-source complexity' – *not* strong-director-telling-us-what-to-do. I asked Kissane to explain how this worked in practice and in the making of the piece:

Jay wasn't trying to say, 'I'm a woman and I know women's stuff so let me tell you women how to do your thing.' He was saying, 'Here's an observation I've made about our society, this is something that troubles me and I want to do a show with it.' I feel like he was surprised sometimes by comments of women in the room. I remember having a conversation with him early on where I said, 'You know this is a terrifying thing, right, this idea of disappearing, you know this is something women face?' He was thinking in terms of Lindsay [Lohan] and Britney [Spears], but these are young women. Yes, we raise them up and yes, they go up in flames, but Dana and I were close to 40 and our reality is that what happens is you go along for a while and all of a sudden you are an old person, meaning over 40, and you are no longer relevant and you are totally marginalized and you completely disappear and that is what is terrifying about [this piece]: having your voice taken away and being banished and you are no longer in charge as others come up

through the ranks. And he was really surprised. So he didn't try to lay his experience on this piece, he gave us space to step into it.
(Interview, 7 August 2014)

The production was feminist because the actors completing their task made it so, not because the concept or director made it so. Kissane and company were answering to the question at the heart of the process, not to the director.

> We were women coming together and having an adventure. We had armies and got to do things we normally don't get to do. There was a lot of space to explore being political, being a leader who is a female without having to be a female leader because all the leaders were female. Something magical happened by giving us parts that were written for men. It just gave us access to more stuff that we could totally do but that wouldn't have occurred to the playwright or to the actors because we still only write *this* kind of female character, even after all this time. I get these kids' books from the library for my daughter and so many of them are, the beginning of the book is like, 'They always told Lucy she couldn't be a pirate but she wanted to be a pirate and so she became a pirate anyway, good for Lucy!' Why do we have to introduce that first part of the story? Why do I have to tell my kid that everyone thinks Lucy can't be a pirate and she did it anyway and that's the world we're still living in? Can't we just have Lucy be the pirate? What's the problem with that?!? But in *Richie* we were all pirates, so we could just be pirates.
> (Interview, 7 August 2014)

The key to the show's success lay less in what was conceptually imposed and much more in what the new context made available. When I noted the apparent irony of this being achieved with a very strong male director at the helm, the women I interviewed noted the qualities of Jaybird's work that are in the devising rather than the more traditional Daddy Director mode.

> With Jay you have to take care of your own shit as an actor. You are responsible for *bringing* to him. He shapes it and takes it farther. He also throws you a lot of ideas but they quickly get discarded. This used to be disorienting for me in the amount of feedback and then contradictions in the feedback, but he's just trying stuff to see: what sticks? What settles? It's a collaboration because it has to settle for both of us in a place that's interesting. He's a skilled follower of what the actors are bringing. There was an initial discussion about the concept but not much

after that. There was lots of time spent on logistics. It was very fulfilling because everyone had to step up to make that work. It was a very independent experience.

(Interview, 7 August 2014)

What was it like that all these women were being directed by a man? I didn't even think about it. Most of us came in with ideas about our characters' behaviours, and Jay helped us decide how far to take things.

(Interview, 10 August 2014)

In devised, company-created work, the director may be instrumental in setting the tasks – he or she is indeed the taskmaster, just not in the pejorative sense we usually mean it now – but the director does not dictate how the tasks are to be carried out. That is what the company does, and the very specific ways in which each member of the company 'completes' the task becomes part of the story within the new structure of the event.

For *Richie*, another interesting dispersal of control and eschewing of the predetermined came with the costume design. The idea was that there would be a head costume designer who then went off to work with four Durham-area clothing designers who then met with each actor individually to determine her character's particular look. During the rehearsal period, each actor came up with her own armour for riding into this production's battles; it was only just before opening that Jay took an overall look and made any final but minor adjustments. This part of the design process seems reflective of the overall creative approach. Shakespeare's play is always there and available as the anchor, and the director is always there and available as instigator and editor, but the event is postdramatic in Lehmann's sense as the manifestation of the company's creative impulses in carrying out the ideas and dealing with the tasks. The director may still work 'choreographically', but not in that traditional sense of coming up with and handing over the blocking. Rather, the director's work is in refining and clarifying the emergent gestural and spatial vocabulary that, again, comes out of the company's efforts in dealing with the tasks.

What is predetermined and what is purposefully unpredictable? Anne Bogart maintains:

> as a director, my job is to propose big, wide and penetrating questions ... my job is to transcend my own agenda in order to see the wider context and my job is to cultivate the kind of spaciousness where permission is possible. I try to create the room in which everyone [practitioners first and audiences later] is both participating and responsible.
>
> (Bogart 2014, 26)

Kissane sees this permissiveness/responsibility in the work of Little Green Pig:

> The actors and the director are having a collaboration but somebody is in charge of 'making sure' ... We do these really risky shows and there has to be a certain faith that this is not going to suck. If we know it's not going to suck then people are willing to take all sorts of risks, knowing that at the end of the day there is an eye there to bring it back.
> 
> (Interview, 7 August 2014)

The risks aren't just off-the-wall, unconnected nonsense, because while giving permission for the unexpected and the unpredictable to occur the director also maintains the ability to see the whole picture and bring it back – to curate the surprises that emerge from messing about with the set tasks in the open form. For Kissane this has become an essential attribute of the work she wants to do or see: 'With LGP there are surprises available, and as a theatregoer I really need that, I need some things that are unexpected to happen ... it's inspiring to be surprised' (Interview, 7 August 2014).

In his *Mis-Directing the Play: An Argument Against Contemporary Theatre*, Terry McCabe tells any practising or would-be directors to remember this simple maxim: 'You are the deliveryman and the play is the package' (McCabe 2001, 38). The metaphor implies that 'the play' is of course already complete in itself – delivery people are not supposed to change what's in the package en route. This sits nicely with David Mamet's thoughts on directing, namely to deliver what the playwright has created without messing it up or breaking it. Directors should know the route, drive carefully, avoid any big bumps and, perhaps, be at the ready to fend off trouble such as thieves, vandals, vagabonds, uppity actors or innovative designers. In devising (with) Shakespeare, the process works a bit differently. The director's responsibility lies more with the time and the place and the people involved. As Peter Brook has said, 'Shakespeare ... is like the real world, it has a looseness, an openness, which goes far beyond the vanity of strict form' (in Croyden 2003, 10). The director's primary relationship to the script is not to somehow serve and protect it in order to deliver it unharmed and intact, but to make sure it remains an open form for this group of practitioners and their audiences to step into and to structure, for their time and place and immediate concerns. As an open form rather than a sealed-up package, available in all its 'open-source complexity' rather than padded and protected for the journey, the script serves the tasks and new context within which it functions and through which it speaks. In the case of *Richie*, Shakespeare's words served this rolling pub crawl of actors and audiences by anchoring, and giving highly expressive voice to, its exploration of celebrity culture in twenty-first-century America. In devising this Shakespeare, the director asked the question and set the task and curated the variety of personal, unexpected and fully committed responses the company provided. Maybe a director still is the deliveryman: he or she 'delivers' the unpredictable. In this case O'Berski, along with the entire company, ensured the 'package' fell off the back of the truck, split open, and made its purposefully tumbling contents available, to the surprise and delight of participants and passers-by up and down the streets.

# 6
# Fixing Shakespeare

Devising is a particular way of looking at making theatre, and it's one that makes good sense to me. It suits my own commitment to cultivating, harnessing and delivering the unpredictable. It's a process that informs how I might make a new work out of, say, interviews with prison inmates, or stories by Edgar Allan Poe, or a script by Shakespeare. I wonder, though, where exactly it stands in relation to the larger, and more traditional, and possibly more vexed, question of adaptation, as well as to the literal definition of the auteur director as writer of the theatrical event (Sidiropoulou 2011, 1–2). Adaptation is, of course, a whole huge subject on its own. From the point of view of getting Shakespeare on to the stage, I want to consider two rather different ways of thinking about that word: adaptation as something *we* do *to* the play, and adaptation as something the play does in its new environment. The first, the *done to*, is what we think about when we change and adapt a novel into a television series, or a comic book into a movie, and so seems suited to talking about how we make a script into a production, some words by Shakespeare into a show. But the second, the more life sciences definition of how a thing changes to become better suited to its (new) environment, also seems useful in thinking about how these plays have remained alive in an ever-shifting art form for so long.

These plays always have to adapt to their new environments, if we believe that they truly are these incredibly rich open forms (with 'open-source complexity'). But they don't just do it on their own – even setting aside for the moment the more active/aggressive notion of doing things to them. Thinking more biologically, they are set up to adapt (or not) based on the complex contingencies of their making, but also on the strength and quality of the questions we are asking of them – the questions we ask will of course influence the stories we are telling and therefore what the play 'does' in the material/social/political context it finds itself in. To return again to conventional notions of directing versus devising, and concepts versus questions: concepts *do to*, they impose upon scripts to shape them into new forms and shape an audience's response; questions *ask of* and, in a sense, give rise to the inclusive new environments that the play, the company and the audiences then adapt to.

We may also think about the two notions of adapting in terms of two different toolkits for the practical work of making theatre. Using writer's tools, we adapt a script by changing its language and/or structure in some way – we change the content, directly, and often right from the outset. Using director's tools, we create, alter or shift the environments the script will function within – we change the context, and let that work on the content, often over the course of rehearsals and even through the run. In both cases, using both toolkits, we are making something else, something other than what we started with. The focus for this chapter is on how these different toolkits work, what kinds of things get done with them, and whether we can arrive at the same ends through radically different means.

One of the tried and true and very oft-used tools in the director's kit is the framing device, but even at its most elegantly streamlined it can involve a bit of rewriting. At the beginning of Cheek By Jowl's now-legendary staging of *As You Like It* (I saw it in 1992 in the Swan in Stratford-upon-Avon), the all-male cast assembled, all in (male) formalwear, and Jacques' most famous line was moved to the top of the show: 'All the world's a stage, and the men' – the actors who would go on to play male characters moved a bit to one side – 'and women' – and the rest moved a bit the other way – 'merely players.' That was enough to effectively rewrite the standard heteronormative Shakespearean comedy into something where gender was put on and desire floated freely. This very briefest of preludes, using a line from the play and a simple but striking image, provided a way of looking at the action that, for me at least, lasted for the rest of the evening and beyond. Chris Abrahams' 2014 *Midsummer Night's Dream* at Stratford, Ontario put a very particular frame around the action by staging the play as a play staged by a group of actors as a wedding gift to celebrate the nuptials of some dear friends. We entered the theatre to a backyard barbecue in full swing and when the guests of honour arrived for curtain time we saw that they were both male. There was much else of interest in the production proper (Lysander was played as female by a woman, Titania was played as female by a man) but the notion of performing this play in loving celebration of a same-sex marriage (the couple was clearly visible through the entire show, and the actors were constantly checking in with them) grounded the action in a contemporary and bittersweet reality – in the culture wars of the early twenty-first century, none would know better than these that the course of true love never did run smooth. Like the Cheek By Jowl *As You*, the frame rewrites/overwrites the entire action of the play, although one of Shakespeare's lines was significantly altered, as Puck assured all present that 'Jack shall have Jill ... Jill shall have Jill ... Jack shall have Jack ... and all shall be well'.

I think the key is that, unlike a particular choice of period or setting – which is probably the most used director's tool – a frame usually isn't naturalized into the action but remains as a way of, a way that we are, viewing the action as a whole. Here's Susannah Clapp in *The Guardian* on the striking and elaborate framing of Phyllida Lloyd's Donmar all-female Shakespeare Trilogy (*Henry IV, Julius Caesar, The Tempest*, 2012–17):

> All are presented as if performed in a prison by inmates: statements by actual prisoners connecting their lives to the stories on stage are read out. Suddenly you see that everyone in *The Tempest* is a captive, physically or emotionally. Suddenly you see that Henry's crown is a jailer. Suddenly these plays are wired unforgettably into the 21st century.
>
> (Clapp 2016)

Contemporaneity – how the stories that a performance makes available strike us right now – seems to come from an awareness of the plays adapting to their new environments. Not just to a concept, which an audience 'gets' in about three seconds and then naturalizes into the unfolding events, and not just to a period setting, which again audiences just accept as when events happen, but to this thing that *is played* and that is *something other* than the plot/characters/events in the script.

Sometimes critics who don't buy into the frame (and don't think the play in question adapts well to it) ask, not unreasonably, why not just do a new play? It's as if the point of view a frame provides on the action somehow no longer merits Shakespeare's words to go with it – so, the director's tools should just be traded for the writer's tools and have at it. Shakespeare performance history is filled with directors seeing how far they can go by pilfering from the writer's kit while ultimately falling back on their own. *The Taming of the Shrew* is an interesting test case here, as it already has a frame on its central action and many productions have (authorially) rewritten the frame in order to set up some particular (directorial) take on the Kate/Petruchio story. Michael Bogdanov (for the RSC in 1978) famously rewrote the induction to have Jonathan Pryce's drunk and irate theatregoer/

Sly/Petruchio abuse Paola Dionisotti's unlucky usher/hostess/Kate before tearing down the faux-Italianate set in preparation for a particularly thoroughgoing examination of toxic masculinity. Bill Alexander tried something different for the RSC in 1992 when his blue-collar Sly fell in with a bunch of cold, calculating and mean-spirited toffs in order to try to make the play proper more about class than sexual politics. Most interestingly, the Chicago Shakespeare Theater, in a production directed by Josie Rourke in 2010, commissioned a writer rather notorious for the examinations of misogyny in his own plays and films to create new framing material that decentred men in the resulting picture. Neil LaBute's new 'Shrew Scenes' framed the play as difficult dress rehearsals wherein a lesbian director and her lover/leading lady worked out the power dynamics of their relationship for all, including us, to see (Di Salvo 2013). In each case new text is meant to serve directorial choices – the two toolkits complement each other, but the director is calling the shots and Shakespeare's text remains substantially intact.

Sometimes the two toolkits just get spilled on the ground and their contents hopelessly mixed up – that seems to be what happened in a piece called *Shakespeare's R&J* by writer/director Joe Calarco. Cary Mazer (in 'Not Not Shakespeare', 2005) has brilliantly teased out the issues and implications involved in this New York hit from the late 1990s where a particular production that Calarco directed in a particular context with four male actors gave rise to a framing device of the actors playing students in an all-male Catholic boarding school who experiment with putting on *Romeo and Juliet*. The adaptation for this production became the script, which now is copyrighted by Joe Calarco even though pretty much every line is still Shakespeare's. The script is a record of the staging's new frame/work, and it's hard to say whether securing the rights to perform it (from Dramatists Play Service) provides a company with a new play, a newly adapted old play, or a play that in this case just comes substantially pre-directed.

Other adaptive work attempts to stick with writer's tools – and just to stick to the dialogue. In 2015 the Oregon Shakespeare Festival began a three-year programme they are calling 'Play on! 36 Playwrights translate Shakespeare'. The company's original press release explains the brief:

> *Play on!* has engaged many of the nation's leading playwrights, dramaturgs, theater professionals, expert advisors and emerging voices in the field. Among the goals of the project is to increase understanding and connection to Shakespeare's plays, as well as engage and inspire theatergoers, theater professionals, students, teachers and scholars. *Play on!* also will provide translated texts in contemporary modern English as

performable companion pieces for Shakespeare's original texts in the hope they will be published, read and adapted for stage and used as teaching tools.

(www.osfashland.org/press-room/press-releases/play-on)

The programme is led by Lou Douthit, Production Dramaturg with over 20 seasons at the Festival. In a lengthy piece she wrote for *HowlRound*, Douthit gets into the mechanics of how exactly each playwright-and-dramaturg pair will 'collaborate' with Shakespeare on their translation:

*First, do no harm.* There is no word for the kind of subtle and rigorous examination of language that I am interested in. 'Translation' is as close as I can find. There is plenty of the language that doesn't need translating. And there is some that does. I expect the equation of this will vary vastly from play to play.

*Second, go line by line.* No editing, no cutting, no fixing, no personal politics, no regionalisms. The story and characters and time period stay the same.

*Third,* and most important, *the language has to retain the same kind of rigor and pressure as the original.* Which means it still has to have rhyme, meter, rhetoric, image, metaphor, character, action, and theme. Shakespeare's astonishingly compressed language must be respected.

The translation is not to be a paraphrase, nor is it a literal explanation of what's going on. The translations are not meant to be replacements of the originals. Our mission with this project is to learn a ton about the plays and to create performable companion pieces. They are new plays in that way.

(Douthit 2015, original emphasis)

The notions put forward here seem endlessly fascinating to me, as far as writer's tools and director's tools are concerned. 'Do no harm' is a reasonable place to start, especially for a Shakespeare festival. The modernized version of the Hippocratic oath implies that something living and breathing is on the writer's table here, but it also begs the question of who gets to define harm and how anyone might recognize when this patient is in distress. It makes me think about *Richie* (see Chapter 5) and the actors in that wild production who all felt they were doing Shakespeare – which they were, because they spoke more 'words by Shakespeare' than will likely be in Oregon's new translations. In fact, there seems something perhaps unintentionally provocative about what these 'new plays' will *not* be. Substitute 'production' for 'translation' (a word Douthit doesn't really like anyway) – 'The [production] is not to be a paraphrase, nor is it a literal explanation of what's going on. The [productions] are not meant to be replacements of the originals.' Surely good productions neither simplify nor explain the script either; so too directing doesn't replace, or efface, or ruin, or destroy Shakespeare's (contribution to the) work. I think that new and interesting productions are a lot like new plays. Perhaps writing new words and writing new events are closer in kind than some notion of two toolkits would allow.

But Douthit is trying to reduce variables so that the work here is done *only* with writer's tools:

> *[T]here will be a dramatist's perspective in the center of these plays for the first time in 400 years.* Typically, we rely on information about the plays from actors, directors, dramaturgs, designers, and scholars. I'm asking the writers to go into the plays ... and see what they discover about how the plays work from within their structure.
>
> (Douthit 2015, original emphasis)

The key here seems to be 'from within their structure' – that would make this project rather different from what playwright Paula Vogel 'discovered' in writing *Desdemona: A Play About A Handkerchief*, or what theatre-maker Young Jean Lee discovered writing *LEAR*: obviously their engagement with Shakespeare's texts didn't stop at some new perspective on the language. Douthit is trying to hold the line, as it were, in going line by line to keep the question of adaptation from expanding beyond measure – in a sense, to try and keep what she is calling translation separate from how we usually think of adaptation on the page or in production:

> We already adapt Shakespeare every time we produce the plays. And by that, I mean that we examine different versions (quarto versus folio), we edit scenes or move them around, we change words that have changed meaning over time, and we adjust language to fit casting choices and production concepts. (In fact, it's a rare production of a Shakespeare play with everything intact.) But I'm curious to see what we learn about the language and how the plays work if we hold all the other variables in place.
>
> (Douthit 2015)

How the plays work at the level of language – that is what this programme, with so many new writers using writer's tools (i.e. changing the words) is meant to explore. It is, one assumes – given so much effort by so many and in spite of Douthit's second commandment above – also meant to fix a few things. After all, Douthit began the whole enterprise because (even after 20-odd years at a major Shakespeare festival) she often found Shakespeare's language to be a problem – 'It can be as foreign to me sometimes as, well, a foreign language' (Douthit 2015). Sometimes, what Shakespeare wrote and the way that he wrote it doesn't work and could use a little fixing.

I fix Shakespeare all the time. There's often quite a lot that just doesn't 'work' for me when I'm putting up a production. But, as Douthit suggests, for a production I rarely limit my variables. Playwrights write words, and they write the structure, and they write the characters who will inhabit that structure and use those words. Depending on the contingencies of production, I may clarify vocabulary and change some words in a line – the kind of fix that would pass muster in the Play on! project – but I may also cut huge numbers of lines, or cut characters, or cut whole scenes, or put scenes in different places, or give lines to different characters, etc. In spite of all that, I always think I am doing Shakespeare, if in fact I think about a question like that at all. However much I use writer's tools to adapt and change things at the level of language and character and structure, I tend to think of that work as part of directing – responding to the situation at hand, working with the actual people and budgets and time that I have, and developing something my audiences can take on board in the moment. When I'm directing I'm not interpreting the writing. I'm trying to figure out how to make something. And I never feel like I am adapting scripts, or like I am some daring auteur, when it all just seems like part of making theatre.

That is the link I'm missing with the writer's work for Play on! If these new 'performable' scripts are not set up to take the place of Shakespeare's and get performed, is it like taking the car to the garage to get fixed and then just leaving it there? Surely fixing the language is meant to make the action more accessible *in the moment* and *in performance* – otherwise SparkNotes or Arden footnotes would do the same job. Perhaps the variables can be reduced from a 'dramatist's perspective' in translating words, but I wonder how much learning about 'how the plays work' can be done if you are not subjecting them, precisely, to the lots and lots and lots of specific variables of even their most conservatively run work environments.

Since 2013, the Austin, Texas theatre collective Rude Mechs has been up to something remarkably similar but done completely differently. Their Fixing Shakespeare project is more overt, and more down and dirty, than their Oregonian counterpart:

> Our new series, Fixing Shakespeare, will make William Shakespeare's least produced works useful again. Ask yourself how many Shakespeare

plays you know or have seen, subtract that number from thirty-seven (depending on who you ask), and those are the plays we are working to fix using our patented performance creation methodology, contemporary English, and adding curse words (Shakespeare cursed plenty, but most Elizabethan curse words have lost their spice. Zounds!). In some ways, we're offering you a more authentic experience of what a new Shakespeare play might be like than an actual Shakespeare play. In other ways, not so much.

(rudemechs.com)

However the Play on! project's 'contemporary modern English' translations turn out, this is what the Rude Mech's 'contemporary English' amounted to in their very first go at it, *Fixing King John*:

**Act I, Scene I.**
*Everything you see is KING JOHN'S castle. And lookit,*
*KING JOHN is on his throne. He looks gooood. He's the*
*home team along with his mom, QUEEN ELINOR, and*
*PEMBROKE, and anyone else you see. Anyone except that*
*slick DAUPHIN, who's on a visit from France.*
KING JOHN
What the fuck? France? Fuck France. What do you want?
Wait. Kneel first and say it again.
DAUPHIN
I can't kneel for what I wanna say. Reason why is – pretend I wasn't his son, but the King of France himself. The words I say are his words, arranged by him to spit a message in your ear. So pretend *you* to be the great King of England and brace yourself, motherfucker.
\*\*\**Oh shit.*
QUEEN ELINOR
What's he mean 'pretend you to be?' There's no pretend to it.
Stand up straight. You're King-Fucking-John of England, so what's he mean?
KING JOHN
I dunno, *Mom*! Let's write him a special letter with our listen-pen.
…
DAUPHIN
Step aside! Stop pretending to be the great King of England, because really-truly it's your nephew, Arfur, who has the most reason to pretend that game. Whoop!

KING JOHN
If Arfur wants my crown he's gonna hafta come back from the grave and chop off my head to get it, 'cause I'll kill a motherfucker today just for scheduling a thought like that tomorrow. Fuck Arfur. Tell Philip that. Then what?
DAUPHIN
Total fucking all-out war. Whoop, whoop!
(Lynn n.d.)

Founding member and Co-producing Artistic Director Kirk Lynn is the one responsible for this foray into Shakespeare using some pretty sharp writer's tools. He arrived at the idea not through some interest in subtle and respectful collaboration but from a desire to create the most brilliant and bad-ass of cover versions:

> I was running and I was listening to a White Stripes live album, and they were covering 'Stop Breaking Down,' by Robert Johnson, and I started thinking, 'Would Robert Johnson even recognize this as his music?' Especially on the live version, not on the album version, the solo is just so aggressive and noisy. I was like, 'I want to do that.' The poet Charles Simic said this thing I really feel connected to. He said that writers want to honor the masters of their craft, but they also want to overthrow them and make room for themselves and sort of destroy them. I thought, 'I just want to cover something and make it sound like the White Stripes make "Stop Breaking Down" sound: respectful, and clearly in the tradition of blues – and loving the blues – but just annihilating it, too.'
> (In Darling 2013)

To honour and annihilate – rather a different mandate from 'first do no harm', although I for one am convinced that Lynn's language retains the 'same kind of rigor and pressure as the original' – that commandment at the heart of the Play on! mandate. The 'patented performance creation methodology' went like this:

> I went online, downloaded the full text as a text file, and every morning before I would start whatever my bigger project was, I would just do a page or so, turning it into contemporary English and adding curse words ... So, that was the first pass. Then, I abandoned any loyalty to the Shakespearean text and just tried to edit it like I would one of my plays: Cut it down to 10 characters so you could do it. *King John* goes from 22 down

to 10 characters. Then, just smooth out the plot. And then there were some other things. I really wanted to push toward more gender parity, so I gave the female characters more lines.

(In Darling 2013)

Lynn *started* with going line by line but the writer's tools seem to give way to director's or producer's tools, because the intent was always for Rude Mechs to actually *do* these new scripts – so they got readings with the company, then workshops, then full productions. Rude Mechs found that their 'translated' Shakespeare worked pretty well, and in a way that the Play on! practitioners would certainly envy: review after review for *Fixing King John* and for their second in the series, *Fixing Timon of Athens*, talk about how vibrant, energetic, engaging and accessible these new/old/fixed and ferociously bad-ass covers turned out to be on stage.

But covers of what, exactly? Is a Play on! script meant to function as a cover version of the *lines*, while Fixing Shakespeare – meant as it is for performance – is a raucous and robust cover of the *action*? Both will see rewritten texts – the overt, systematic and thoroughgoing use of writer's tools – but one goes note-for-note and the other is … what? More in the spirit of the thing? Speaking as a director, *Fixing King John* strikes me as exactly how I would want *King John* to feel and sound in performance. Do we expect cover versions to 'work' because of their close relation to some brilliant original, or because they make free and original use of a source to create more and new art? With the perfect cover, are we enthralled by the echoes or the newness? That can be a hard response to untangle. When I first read the script of *Fixing King John* I thought that perhaps going all-in with writer's tools, at least as wielded by someone like Lynn working for a company like Rude Mechs, just might be the best way to make a case for Shakespeare. Then, in the most unexpected place, I experienced a company achieving what felt like exactly the same thing without changing a single word of Shakespeare's text.

When you spend a weekend at a major classical theatre company seeing *King Lear* at the matinee and *King John* in the evening and you come away thinking that *King John* is clearly the better play, something must be up. That's what happened to me while visiting the Stratford Festival in Ontario in 2014. With *King Lear*, the lines were spoken clearly as incident followed incident, I distinctly remember being alert and awake, but I had no idea what was going on. It was quite startling, this feeling that nothing made any sense, to the point where the basic plot almost becomes inaccessible (perhaps I mean unnecessary) because there seems no reason why the figures on stage are doing *this* thing as opposed to some *other* thing they could be doing. Reason not the need indeed. I could have chalked this up to my own rather long history of being chronically uninspired by the vast majority of what I see from so-called major theatre companies, were it not that three hours after the curtain came down on that show I found myself at another production where suddenly every single word, every single incident and every single character interaction made perfect, and perfectly contemporary, sense – every moment of the way through.

At least a few things about Stratford's *King John* might not have promised such a result. It was done in Elizabethan dress, on a bare stage, and with something of an Original Practices aesthetic – none of which scream 'contemporaneity' from the start. For me, the more overt staging elements from the Original Practices playbook, like some odd period pronunciations, and the company dance at the end, and what appeared to be the steadily dimming lights to approximate candles burning down, just seemed annoyingly affected. But while a few of the staging practices gestured at some historical origins, the sensibilities that came through in the playing were completely contemporary – the tone of voice, the edgy and idiosyncratic body language, all the acid-dripping looks and smiles. Where Lynn translated Shakespeare's lines so that the action's almost continuous sense of 'Fuck you/You're a fucking idiot/I am going to fuck you up' was apparent in the written (curse)words, the Stratford company delivered almost every line – cheekily, viciously – so that Shakespeare's words felt exactly the same way. These actors appeared to simultaneously translate the subtext as clearly as Rude Mechs (re)wrote it on the page, but they just really seemed to need *these* (the 'original') words to do it.

If the director wasn't using writer's tools, or a framing device, or a radical resetting, how did this *King John* come across with such contemporaneity while *King Lear* seemed so old and impenetrable? Tim Carroll is best known for his work at the Globe Theatre with Mark Rylance – although in the future his fate will be tied to the Shaw Festival in Niagara-on-the-Lake, Ontario, where he has at the time of writing just taken over as artistic director. He worked on a number of Original Practices productions at the Globe, but has also done some major productions elsewhere – a *Merchant of Venice* at the RSC in 2008, a *Romeo and Juliet* at Stratford, Ontario in 2013, the season before his *King John*. We might, reductively if not altogether inaccurately, think of Original Practices (OP) work as 'text-centred', but while the text may be at the centre much depends upon the angle from which we view it and the direction from which we approach it. Carroll espouses what at first sounds like a kind of directorial neutrality – indeed, many of the reviews for the 2008 *Merchant* took to task a kind of studied lack of inflection and interpretation in the piece. In an interview before *King John* this neutrality comes off a bit banal: 'I'm very interested in what happens when you let the play speak for itself, even if in the end that's impossible and you can't help imposing something' (in O'Connor 2014). However, much depends on the angle from which you view this notion. Carroll has provided elsewhere a much more detailed perspective and hardly a neutral point of view on his particular methodology. The key to what Carroll achieved for me with *King John* lies not in the OP Globe work but in the work he did, starting in England in 2007, with actors in a small-scale collective training/performance group calling itself The Factory.

The sheer amount of process material available on The Factory's community blog (thefactory.wikifoundry.com) is extraordinary. Briefly: the project was designed for a group of actors to meet regularly to improve their craft. The inspiration was more sports team than theatre school, and performers would not be working on 'the production' but on exercises, obstructions and tasks that would enhance their abilities to respond, with a text, to whatever changes of circumstances might befall them, i.e. to whatever might happen to their squad out there on the field. Their first project used *Hamlet*, but the process is more important than the particular play: they weren't 'doing' *Hamlet* so much as doing the process, with *Hamlet* serving as the script. Here's how Carroll initially explained the impulse for the work:

> How much an actor needs to decide, or think, or agree with a director on such things as character, motivation and even narrative are, it goes without saying, questions that one could debate at great length. It's a debate that, if we get this project off the ground, I am sure we will have, and I look forward to it. But it is only fair to point out that the project itself will radically circumscribe that debate. The reason it will do so is one of the reasons I am so passionately attached to this method: it has a kind of built-in veto on *interpretation*. Not that I have anything against interpretation *per se*; I just don't really think it's our job.
>
> (Carroll 2006, original emphasis)

Interpretation is not the director's or the actor's job. Their job is to keep making new things by figuring a way through whatever is presenting itself in the moment – a different actor in the role opposite, a change in location, other tasks or new instructions. Their responses are hardly random. They are not building a role or an interpretation but they are building skills and 'new' performing muscles and an understanding of how to use them:

> How can one have an actors' forum that is both catholic and, at the same time, has an unmistakeable *direction* to its work? The answer is

that the manager of a [sports] team can afford to bring in a new coach to take training one day without the team feeling that they are being confused or led off in a different direction. The new coach may have a different philosophy: this is called a refreshing change. Likewise, a director invited to work with our group for the first time might have a very specific interpretation; why should this be a problem? I can't actually imagine a session or rehearsal that could seriously scupper our preparations to play, for one simple reason: *everything gets thrown away.* This is the principle of the show, and therefore of the rehearsal: whatever happens, however brilliant, it happens only once. Whatever insight is gained into character, no matter how blinding the revelation, it is not discussed again and nothing is built on it – except, inevitably and healthily, in a subterranean way.

(Carroll 2006, original emphasis)

The job isn't to push through or past those things and keep doing what you are 'supposed to' be doing – a certain way of speaking the lines, a set characterization, yesterday's discoveries and decisions – but to deal with, to *play*, whatever is new and different as it becomes part of the story *now*. Early on they did a lot of listening-without-attitude exercises, and that seems indicative. As an actor, one doesn't arrive in the scene already playing a predetermined response – an interpretation – to an interaction that hasn't happened yet. This is not the same as being neutral, as the skill developed is an ability to listen as if what you are listening to, as you are listening to it, actually matters.

As a training company rather than a production company, they were working on building muscles and skill sets rather than with the usual focus on making the show better. Here's Carroll much later in the *Hamlet* blog, after the group had been working together and giving one-off performances for quite a time:

There is indeed a great deal more to be mined from playing Hamlet the way we first set it up. We certainly haven't mastered the form: our audiences' reactions demonstrate how far we are from getting it right every time. The instinct to keep at it until we get it right is a sound one. But, sound instinct though it may be, it is the devil who wants us to follow it. The point of this project is not to get anything right; it is to move beyond our comfort zone. You might well think that you are nowhere near reaching that point with the show as it is at the moment; that doesn't matter. If any part of the group is comfortable (and some of you are, including some who think they aren't), it is time to move on. It is time to move on even before anyone reaches comfort. That's right. Getting better at the thing we are doing is not the point; the point is moving on into what we know we can't do. And finding that we can. And moving on again. Thus I want everyone to be ready for more tasks and surprises. More suicidal obstructions. More failure. More exhilaration.

(Carroll 2008)

Actors and directors often get focused on what works – a particular moment that has a particular effect. But what is actually working is the methodology in play for getting to those moments – hence the focus on building the skills but throwing the moments away in a 'show' that was a never-ending improvisation on the set script. One learns to fish by catching, not by showing off the catch. There is a strong similarity here to advice Anne Bogart likes to give: don't become attached to results, and the moment you feel attached to something, go on to something else.

The focus on adding obstructions in both the training and performances (and it was obviously quite the focus, judging from plenty of questioning and push-back recorded in the blogs) is about avoiding getting comfortable with things you know how to do, like some notion of 'the play' as a set thing. Actors are still supposed to speak the lines and tell the story, but it has to be in a new way given the arbitrary/challenging/banal obstructions they would face at every rehearsal as well as whenever they performed. There could be no autopilot – the training was about keeping responsiveness part of the day to day of performing, and so staying outward-directed and task-orientated all the time. Faced with new and constantly changing obstructions, actors have to (re)make things up as they go along, and the lines simply have to function in their new environment (we're going to move to a different space for the second half, you can only speak when in physical contact with someone else, you must always start your lines before the other person has finished theirs, etc.).

And here the received wisdom of what it means to 'make the text your own' falls away, if that notion had anything to do with interpreting it, controlling it or becoming comfortable with it. A couple of years into the process one of the actors had such an epiphany:

We talk about 'making the text our own' and I myself have a personal issue which is highly neurotic, never mind useless – an imagined battle with an adopted culture standing between me and the Work of the Great One. But this is all so much cant. All we need to do (and we *do* do more than sometimes) is need the words. Dare to need *these* words in *that* order, using *that* iambic or prosaic structure ... And now I conjure my favourite [Tim Carroll] phrase to date... about being 'odd to ourselves'.

By daring to use *these* words, Shakespeare's words and *only* these words, not our own spare words which are comfy and come straight from our own living-rooms, we paradoxically court that sensation that this play which we all now know so well, has become weird to us. That the words coming out of our mouth are not our own (yes, there's the paradox) – and we are running downhill before a brakeless train gathering speed and there ain't a fucking thing we can or would do to save ourselves except keep running without looking back.

('Federay' 2008)

The job is not to make things work but to keep trying – try it out, let it go, keep running, keep trying. They were using the practical tools of devising to create not a traditional run but something more like a series of one-off performances of the same script. For actors at The Factory, this attitude and training created (apparently more often than not) a brilliant displacement – onto the other people in the scene, onto the task at hand, and onto the audience: 'It has been revelatory to think in terms of the actor being a catalyst/enabler in the audience's creative response to a scene, as opposed to being someone who merely serves up a previously-prepared solution.' (Forum, 23 May 2007, thefactory.wikifoundry.com)

Rude Mechs' *Fixing King John* worked for me because a skilled theatre-maker was doing the translating, but what he was translating was not so much Shakespeare's words as one very particular (and, for me at least, very compelling) version of every character's intent that serves to drive the action. All that subtext was then fixed – in both senses, made better and set – in a new script that honoured and annihilated the original. If the years of training and performance experiments recorded, analysed and debated in The Factory's website is anything to go on, Carroll's *King John* worked for me because his directing strategy also creates a new script – by refusing to serve a prepared solution or interpretation of it. The actors' playfulness and their contemporary sensibilities – clearly visible through the 'period' trappings – enabled me to translate along with them in the moment. After I read all of The Factory's materials, I looked again at that interview Carroll gave while working on *King John* and I found he was saying exactly that:

> Unlike quite a lot of directors, I never give any of that kind of [pre]direction at the beginning. I never do a talk about what I think the play is about. I don't want to tell the actors what it is they're doing. I just want to start and see where we get to and find out ... Ideally what I require of the actors is that they train so that the play can work out differently every time they play it, so that the play can work itself out in the moment.
> 
> (In O'Connor 2014)

In other words: so that the play can adapt and become something new.

One of my earliest professional gigs was directing a show for Pittsburgh's New Works Festival, where new, unproduced one-act plays were given full, if minimalist, productions for a short run. It was author/writing-centred in a way, even though everything else was also new: a new set, new actors, new characterizations, etc. Perhaps that is the genius of the festival's name: new works rather than new plays. But new work is what directors are trying to make regardless of the script, and when it 'works' that's what an audience perceives, as my friend and frequent collaborator – and *Richie* director – Jaybird O'Berski puts it:

> People have been saying to me for years with our Shakespeare productions – and I'm sure you get this with yours as well – they say something like 'Wow, what you did was so clear and accessible, it's like I understood it for the first time, because you really got rid of all the old Shakespeare language that I could never follow.' And I have to tell them, 'No, actually – we changed some words here and there to get rid of completely obscure vocabulary or to make a line fit better with the general setting, but really it's pretty much all what Shakespeare wrote.'
> (Interview, 29 December 2016)

As a director adept in using writer's tools, I can change the lines, and that can make things work better. Because of the privileges and latitude afforded the modern director (and even the most workaday auteur), I can 'do' things in my new covers of old plays – cut, restructure, add a frame, eliminate characters, any and all the fixes that would amount to new authorship in adapting *between* mediums – and still keep Shakespeare's name above the title. And at the level of process, based in the rehearsal room, I can set up an environment with a new perspective, compelling task or impossible obstruction, inhabit it with a group of actors used to, even good at, being outward-directed and in-the-moment, then invite an audience with a taste for the unpredictable, and I can get a clear, accessible, surprising new play that way too.

# 7
# My Year of Shakespeare

During the writing of this book, I set myself a practical challenge: I programmed a Year of Shakespeare celebration at the University of Pittsburgh campus in Bradford where I work. This was partly to commemorate the 450th anniversary of Shakespeare's birth – at least that's what I put in the season brochure. It was mostly to immerse myself in a range of Shakespearean problems that I could then write about. I planned to direct student productions of *A Midsummer Night's Dream* – not a play I had ever given any thought to directing before – for the fall, and of Young Jean Lee's *LEAR* – an adaptation of *King Lear* without Lear, among many other things, and with some radical rethinking both of Shakespeare's play and of what plays in general are supposed to do – for the spring. I also programmed a visit from a Chicago company whose specialty is 'improvised Shakespeare'. When I hatched this plan, I didn't know that the first piece of business would involve an extended road trip to Durham, North Carolina. There, I would be keeping the bench warm, keeping the fires burning, keeping the faith, and keeping the work going in any other way while not-exactly-directing a good friend's production of *Hamlet* over the first half of its rehearsal period when he had to be out of the country. What follows is an account of some of what went on, and some of what I learned from the madness, over four shows from July 2014 to April 2015.

**Directing Without a Director, Directing Without a Production:** Little Green Pig planned to open their 2014–15 season with a minimalist production of Shakespeare's *Hamlet* that they were calling *hmlt*. I had just directed *Celebration (Festen)* with them in April, and Artistic Director Jaybird O'Berski asked then if I (being a Shakespeare person and all that) would like to come to town for a few days during the rehearsal period for this late-summer show to help the company with some text coaching. That's what we set up – until summer came and I heard from Jaybird that an unforeseen scheduling conflict with his actor playing Hamlet clashed badly with a scheduling conflict of his own when he was booked to be in China for two weeks teaching improv. He asked if I could extend my visit – and my brief – by coming down for a couple of weeks and helping to lead rehearsals while he was out of the country. By the time the show opened, I was named as the assistant director in the programme, but at the beginning the job description sorted out over the phone was something like this: rehearse the actors for the first two weeks of a four-week schedule, concentrate on text and relationships, don't worry about 'the production' but have them in their stride by the time Jaybird got back.

Instead of thinking that *doing* all the things a director does for half the rehearsal period without *being* the director might be problematic for all involved, I instead thought: sounds good! I wondered if this could be a kind of Original Practices experiment of figuring things out together without a guiding or imposing or stifling directorial presence – not so much *this* particular director, who I've known and worked with for a very long time and with whom I share more or less the same artistic brain but *The* Director, the figurehead, the position, the artistic focal point of decision making in the rehearsal room. It would also mean playing freely with a group of really good actors without the distractions (or the safety nets) of all the elements of modern production: all the design and tech, etc. With this book in mind, I decided to blog through the rehearsal process, to examine every day what we got up to and what it meant to be doing this work without the director and without the production elements. What follows is every entry through those two weeks in 2014, taken directly from a members-only Wordpress blog I set up for the company to view and comment on. After the blogging, I'll follow up with what really happened.

<u>28 July. Jaybird's *hmlt* Hunches – before his departure to China ...</u>
- Definitely modern dress and since we lost our costume designer I'd like you to think about what your character should wear. We can purchase items or pay you back for what you go out and find. Setting is USA 2014, not Denmark or any other period.
- I'm interested in exploring the idea of adoption as subtext. While we'll never make it explicit to the audience I think there's an initial betrayal for adopted children that takes a lifetime to unpack and heal, if it ever does. I'd like to work under the assumption that Hamlet and Ophelia are both adopted (not Laertes) and that their

parents have been loving and supportive but ultimately alienating. The crazy turn of events with the possible murder of King Hamlet (and it should be debatable until late in the play whether Claudius is guilty or Hamlet is just paranoid and seeing/hearing things) exacerbates Hamlet's simmering rage and anxiety that he doesn't belong to this world. Same with Ophelia, whose father is Trans-? (Laurie [now Dale Wolf, playing Polonius], you decide what's up here) and identifies as male. The nature of the other missing partner can be debated. I think Laertes should be a birth child to Polonius or adopted from another family so there's more possibility of sexual attraction between Polonius' kids. Ditto with Hamlet and Gertrude, which I never really buy when he's her birth son but an attraction to an adopted son could be juicy. Or not something we want to explore. Who knows?
- The style should be very naturalistic and yet embody the poetry in a robust, visceral way.

30 July. Kevin's Three Questions for Acting Shakespeare
1) What are you saying? Paraphrase the content specifically and exactly 'in other words' and then return to thinking about why you need <u>these</u> specific words to say it.
2) Why are you there? Everyone needs a reason to be in a scene, so, what do you want and how are you trying to get it?
3) What are you doing? What is the physical narrative of movement and stillness, gesture, spatial relations, and reasonable and revealing physical actions?

2 August. Viewpointing
Can text work be radically different from traditional table work? Dana and I kind of think so. While our first two weeks will focus on making the text work in useful ways, neither of us feels that is best done, uhm, seated. Meaning in Shakespeare is best tested in action. Dana [Marks, LGP Managing Director, also playing Horatio] and I are both pretty invested in Viewpoints work – perhaps some of you are too. Even if that way of working is new to you, the great thing about the Viewpoints is that they are things you are doing anyway, things like playing with the speed of your movements, or radically altering how close to or far away from other characters you can get, or discovering the gesture that feels right for the way your character shakes hands or feels about being watched. Sometimes (and I say this as a card-carrying academic) the footnotes at the bottom of the

page in the Arden edition are less 'revealing' than, say, playing with stillness, or following someone when they're not looking. Working this way, we're building the physical narrative at the same time as we're parsing the words – wherever we find the scent, that's what we'll follow.

<u>4 August. While yet of this rehearsal my memory is still green</u> [working on Act I, Scene ii]
At any given moment, what is going on? Sure, Claudius is talking to the gathered parties about marrying Gertrude. But why? What is going on? And that's where actions are so important. He's got some words. What are they meant to do? Maybe he's just asserting his new authority. Or maybe he is reassuring everyone about the course they've all embarked upon. If it's that one, the simultaneous job is to make sure the lines can actually express what might be going on. If he's trying to reassure, then certain operative terms pop out, like 'discretion' because we all know that's a good thing, right, just like 'better wisdoms', and what's even better than better wisdoms but better wisdoms 'freely' given?! Certain appositions or antitheses become necessary – we honor HIM by thinking of OURSELVES. A pause in a good spot so a thought hangs there for a moment, or a quick movement through some phrases or even whole lines so you can get to the thing that really counts … whatever it is from a technical standpoint that you can marshal and organize so that the words start to SOUND LIKE what is actually going on, SOUND LIKE what you want them to DO. And then there are the physical things that seem to come out of the lines but also make sense of the lines, of what is going on, of why anyone is doing anything. So Gertrude nods knowingly to Claudius while glancing at her son, and suddenly it's crystal clear that Claudius is talking to Hamlet because Gertrude wants him to, they've talked about this already, behind his back and in another room, they are a team of concerned parents, and if Hamlet sees that little nod, then he knows they've been talking about him and they've come up with something that they think is best for him, never mind what he actually might be thinking or feeling or whatever. So then what does he do? Stand there and take it? Maybe. Then all that stillness sets him up to explode when he wishes he could JUST FUCKING MELT INTO THE FUCKING GROUND!!! And then we know exactly what it means and what it feels like when he decides the only way to get by is to hold his tongue again.

5 August. 'Welcome to Elsinore ...'
What is playable?
One of the amazing things about rehearsal is getting ideas out of our heads and into the room: you have a notion, and then you have to find out whether that notion can register outside of your internal thought process. Shakespeare makes that seem even trickier, because of all the words, words, words that always threaten to constrain the 'action' of a scene to the opening and closing of your mouth ...
Last night's rehearsal was chock full of playable things:

'I've got a boner and that's not good.' [Laertes greets his sister]
'I am the BEST student in this classroom!' [Ophelia works to impress her dad]
'Oh, sweetie, let daddy explain: that's what we call love!' [Polonius understands his daughter's Hamlet problems]
'You want some acting? Okay, lemme find my light ...' [Player King is a pro, son, just watch]
'Welcome to Elsinore ... I'm the resident asshole.' [Hamlet knows his place]

Finding the playable, to me at least, means that then the words, words, words sound like people talking – conniving, panicking, condescending, working things out – instead of like Shakespearean Actors Acting Shakespeeeaaaaaahhh ...

6 August. Ditching the Baggage
What we bring into the room is just as important as what Shakespeare brings into the room. How could it not be? Shakespeare wrote the script, but we've got to make the production. We bring our bodies, our ways of speaking, our sense of humor, our perspectives on the world – that's a lot to play with.

Some of what we bring in kind of hamstrings our work until we can get past it. Our inherited sense of what Shakespeare is 'supposed to be' or is 'supposed to sound like' – that can be paralyzing, or can lead us into opening our mouths and sounding like John Gielgud in the 1940s (which was great for Gielgud in the 40s but maybe not so much for us). Last night, working on Ophelia, I was very much aware of my baggage. In a way, it's 'good' baggage that comes from years of feminist theory in grad school, but that doesn't mean it is good or useful for helping to figure out what this character is dealing with and where she is coming from and what her options are in terms of the action in the play.

With Claudius, moral judgment can be constipating. I like instead the notion that Claudius didn't kill his brother because he's 'evil' but because he had good reasons and because his becoming king is a good idea. Talk about then adding fuel to Hamlet's fire: if everyone else could see that Claudius is an evil bastard then Hamlet's work would be half done, but the problem is that everyone likes him and he's doing a great job and so it looks like he's gonna get away with it.

The hardest thing in last night's rehearsal was coming up against maybe the most famous speech in all world drama. 'To be or not to be ...' – its reputation rather precedes it. But what is it doing there? What is going on during those famous words? We bring one kind of baggage in with us – the overblown reputation and sense of importance and the echoing-but-for-the-moment-empty words. Maybe we really need to bring in something else to blow that up. WWJD – What Would Jaybird Do? Try the speech as a demented stand-up routine? Deliver the whole thing while executing an elaborate erotic tango with Ophelia? What is going to blow it up so we can start over and start fresh?

7 August. Ask and Ye Shall Receive
Jaybird can't actually access the blog while he's in China but he and I have shared a wavelength for a while now so, not surprisingly, this just in:

'Fever Dream #84: Hamlet doing To Be Or Not a la Reggie Watts on a beat making sound system. That is all.'

And if you are wondering what this means, check out 'Why Shit So Crazy?!?' [Watts' 2010 stand-up comedy special] on Netflix. And imagine the phrase 'to be or not to be' on an endless loop ...

7 August. Echo, Floor Pattern, Repetition, and the Seven Levels of Tension
There was an amazing moment just at the end of rehearsal last night that I didn't have enough time to process before our 10pm stop, so here goes now. At the very end of the Ghost's, uhm, entreaties? orders? to Hamlet, there was a moment of incredible tension where Hamlet was frozen in place, the Ghost all up in his shit, telling Hamlet what to do ... and then the stage suddenly cleared – the Ghost stormed off, Horatio ran after it, and Hamlet was left like a stone statue in the middle of the space. And then he cried out 'OOOOOOOOOOO ...'

And I thought, huh, I've seen and heard this before.

A few rehearsals ago, but only moments earlier in play time, Claudius got all up in Hamlet's shit, telling him what to do, Hamlet was under the enormous stress of biting his tongue, the stage suddenly cleared, and Hamlet was left like a pillar of rock in the middle of the space. And then he cried out 'OOOOOOOOOOO ...'

'O that this too too solid flesh would melt!' 'O all you host of heaven! O earth! What else?'

I love a good echo.

We kind of knew it in that earlier rehearsal, when we talked about the dueling adoptive dads, but it's another thing to see it and hear it and feel it. The echo of an action – the repetition of tension, floor pattern of exits, momentary isolation – and the trap Hamlet is in became palpable: one sharp jaw is Claudius and the sudden new normal, the other is Old Hamlet and his baying for blood, and all Hamlet can do is scream. And both times poor Horatio walks in on it ...

The exercise Dana did last night, of moving closer or farther away based on whether you liked what you were hearing/saying or if you didn't like it, works really well in conjunction with this other exercise I just read about (I think it's a Lecoq thing that comes via Complicite). In this exercise, you are meant to explore with your body the two ends of the scale of muscular tension. Zero might be collapsing and just breathing – we might call it catatonic. Seven is pretty intense, you may only be able to achieve it in certain positions, you may be breathing very shallowly or not at all, and you can't hold it for long – we might call that petrified. And then in between is a scale, each one graded somewhere between those two extremes. Going along with if you think something being said is good or bad in your head, how does it strike you in your body – does it make you more tense or less? Is Hamlet listening to the Ghost a seven, petrified? Is Hamlet listening to Claudius at the wedding reception a six, might we call that simmering rage? Is Ophelia running in to tell Polonius of her silent encounter with Hamlet a five, might that be called something like suspense? Does Polonius inherit Ophelia's five, or does he counter with an alert four? When Polonius figures it out, does he drop to a two-and-a-half, relaxed and economical? When Ophelia gets into the description, or when she realizes she's been a good girl and it's not her fault, does she drop down into relaxed? And so on. Last night Dan [Oliver, Player King] schooled us all, especially Hamlet, by coming in at a relaxed two, immediately jumping to a passionate six for the Hecuba speech, and in a split second dropping back to two when a call came in on his cell that he just had to take. And that was fake. What if the action gave you a motive and a cue for passion?

## 8 August. Realism and Formalism, or, What Works Is What Works
What is the Way of the Pig?

I had a lovely long chat yesterday with LGP Company Member Tamara Kissane. It was mostly about an earlier LGP production, but we also talked about what makes LGP the company that it is. The equation that began to form was something like:

(Risk + Faith) × The Unexpected = LGP.

Ensemble work is conducted in an atmosphere of faith that the risky stuff won't suck which then allows us (and our audiences) to ditch the usual, the regular, the expected: that feels like the LGP way of doing things.

That was certainly borne out for me last night, when we took Jaybird's Beat Box 'To be or not' idea and put it into practice, using Dana, JaMeeka [Holloway-Burrell, Stage Manager], Caitlin [Wells, playing Ophelia] and myself as the four recording tracks of Hamlet's decidedly low-tech machinery [we worked out a system of taps on the head for each of us to repeat a line, stop and start, or 'record' and repeat another line to layer the speech on top of itself]. The speech suddenly started to FEEL like something – it gained a series of rhythms and counterpoints, words popped out, disappeared, reappeared again, certain phrases looped while other ideas rushed forward, and the whole thing suddenly seemed ACTIVE as well as clear. Not exactly a psychological-realist 'solution' – but who says that's where we have to find all our answers? And then, with no contradiction or weirdness that I could perceive, we went straight into the nunnery stuff, which became much more emotionally nuanced and 'realistic' to the point where Hamlet and Ophelia's battle for the microphone [Hamlet was using it to 'announce' his misgivings about Ophelia and her intentions] landed as something both frighteningly violent and overwhelmingly sad.

## 10 August. Inspiration
A shout-out to Jade [Arnold, playing Hamlet] for adding in extra work on Friday – a couple of hours of bashing away at some of the soliloquies. One of the later ones got cut to the bone – now that we know what the action is, we don't need the verbiage and repetitions. Some of the earlier ones are now in that stage of moving away from doing them by instinct and instead breaking them into precisely considered beats, with clear thoughts and deftly marked shifts. Afterwards he said his brain was hurting but in a good way. I said to him that the only note of any real importance he was likely to get from me

through the early process was this: let Hamlet sound like Jade, rather than Jade 'acting' some notion of what anyone else might think Hamlet should sound like.

11 August. Mistakes to the Heart
For those of you who missed last night's four-and-a-half minute long wordless greeting between Hamlet and his excellent good friends Rosencrantz and Guildenstern ... It was a thing of beauty to watch people in the same space inhabiting different universes. It was, of course, a mistake, as Jade didn't realize he had the first line. But as we all know, mistakes can be revealing. The whole thing was weird, off-putting, and absolutely hilarious. Much of it transferred to the scene once we all, ahem, started to do the lines.

Why was this such a productive error and perfectly appropriate mistake? Something about the non-communication, the two-worlds-same-space thing rang absolutely true to what we've been finding as we trace the action of this play. I thought of Polonius and how Dale is playing lower stakes in the surety that the whole problem is about young folks in love. I thought about Ophelia, sheltered and very much used to being the overachiever in a very, very limited world – and then suddenly and irrevocably finding herself in a bigger, scarier, meaner universe. I especially thought about Claudius. Here's a guy who operates in a world of cold-blooded murder, but who wants to live in, who goes about creating and in fact getting other people to live in, a world where it's all cool and everything is okay. And then there's Hamlet. Two-worlds-same-space is I think key to Jaybird's ideas about Hamlet's resentment, his unavoidable position of seeing and feeling most acutely what others are (willfully? ignorantly?) blind and oblivious to – Hamlet as the guy with no eyelids, as someone once described the character.

At some point, of course, there is only going to be one world in that space.

And not everyone is going to be able to live there.

12 August. Obstacles, Resistance, Action
Anne Bogart talks a lot about resistance as an essential element of creativity. She means it in big picture terms – not enough money, not enough time, difficult material, etc. – but also in terms of what an actor deals with moment by moment in the play. What are you up against in a scene? Part of the actor's work is to welcome resistance and obstacles as a 'creative ally.' Identifying and using the obstacles

allow you to concentrate the expression of your action to meet that resistance. No one wants to just be going 'blah blah blah' stuck in one note until the end of a scene. Or worse: inventing arbitrary vocal shifts and changes to make things more 'interesting' but that aren't actually keyed to anything specific. So: what are you up against, where, how much? And how do you meet it?

Last night's rehearsal seemed to be all about resistance. When Horatio and Gertrude walked in just having a conversation, it seemed like a bit of exposition until we got to the real action. When Gertrude played 'I don't want to hear this' suddenly Horatio had something to push against, so her thoughts took on some urgency and some operative words began to stand out to make her point. When Horatio's argument became clearer and more forceful, then Gertrude had something to overcome to get to the point where she could say 'let her come in.'

For Hamlet confronting his mother, alone, for the first time in the play, what a list of obstacles: she immediately takes Claudius' side – in his rage he commits the murder he had been resisting – he murders the wrong person – his mother thinks he's snapped – the Ghost reappears and tells him he's doing it all wrong – apparently his mother can't see the fucking Ghost which must make him look completely fucking crazy in her eyes – and there's still a dead body just outside the room. I'm sure there's more. Each one has to be met, acknowledged, accepted and dealt with in some specific way in the course of moving on. It is not possible to 'move on' as if none of those things are there. Moving on without them makes the scene one-note ('I'm angry!') and incoherent, because the action is not anchored to the ever-changing moment. An AWESOME undertaking – awesome as in huge, and awesome as in totally cool and this is why it's so much fun to get to do this work! We scratched the surface here last night – more soon?

With Ophelia, there's a kind of meta-obstacle to get past first. People call it 'the mad scene' – what the hell is that? You can't just 'be' mad, and you sure as hell can't make a scene out of that. Surely she's doing something! So what are some of her obstacles? Condescension, pity, 'oh well, we know, poor thing' – anything that can allow her to be dismissed. How can that help concentrate the action? It was a brilliant moment last night when Claudius' understanding/condescending 'Conceit upon her father' was met with a searingly concentrated expression of 'Fuck you!' Same with the sex song – as we went on and Caitlin chose her moments to land specific things, it became dangerous/horrifying/embarrassing/funny and most importantly outward-directed. It was more about the world she sees around her, and less about her individual pathology.

And while, of course, everything will change and alter and develop, I really loved finding some resistance to Gertrude's reportage of Ophelia's death. Ophelia died offstage. What is happening here, onstage? I loved the pincer effect of what we started to find: utter non-responsiveness from Laertes in front of her, and Claudius glaring bullets into her back. That speech started to become more interesting and active as Gertrude tried to deal with both of those unexpected things.

13 August. Dem Bones, Dem Bones, Dem Dry Bones
Time to sit in the dirt and play with bones. With Marleigh [Purgar-McDonald, then 11 years old, playing the Gravedigger with a crazy gravelly voice] and Jade clowning in the grave and improvising a Tom Waits tribute band, I started seeing things. I thought of another Shakespearean clown, a decidedly sad one, flinging himself (herself in LGP's case a couple of years ago) on the ground to tell sad stories of the death of kings. I thought of Robin Williams [who had killed himself two days earlier] in the quick riffs and wordplay and comedy and death. And finally I thought that old academic saw –'Is Hamlet just pretending to be mad or is he really mad?!?' – made a kind of sense. With everything else that's going on, sitting in the dirt and playing with bones seemed a bit crazy. And it was also the first time I'd seen Hamlet happy. In a grave, with a strange old man/child, talking about the great levelers dust and death. A strange and rich moment.

14 August. Opening Can After Can of Worms
Rehearsals are always productive, but not always in ways we might immediately recognize. Sometimes it feels like you move from insight to insight, with each insight anchored to some specific word or line that suddenly pops, or to a gesture or physical interaction that suddenly 'makes sense of things.' Sometimes it feels like you are just opening can after can of worms – a wriggling mass of things that you're not sure what to do with and that leaves you vaguely uncomfortable. It can be hard to trust in that teeming chaos of too-much.

Working on that one-page scene between Gertrude and Claudius (after the death of Polonius) last night, it did feel like we'd opened a can of worms with all the possibilities that got brought up. How is Gertrude processing the scene before this, is she thinking about what Hamlet said or about what he did and in what proportion, what is she looking for from Claudius and does she get it, if not then what?

When does Claudius start making decisions and how: is he seizing a golden opportunity, is he trying not to overplay his hand with Gertrude, does he want to be sure of her or is he already moving past her? I'm not sure anything got 'sorted out' by the time we moved on to the next bit of rehearsal, but then something interesting happened.

Actually, lots of interesting things happened in the scene with Ophelia's North-Northwest madness – more clarity and precision, and the isolation of Laertes I think worked really well: it explained why he knew something was very wrong, it made the kiss at the end very disturbing, and it left him totally open and vulnerable to Claudius' moves. But the thing I found most interesting had to do with Gertrude. It's really easy to 'read' those lines Claudius has about 'let him go, Gertrude' and 'leave him, Gertrude' as about Claudius and Laertes and how Claudius starts to handle Laertes and this volatile situation. It is easy enough for Gertrude to get stranded and forgotten. But Claudius is also 'handling' Gertrude here. When Jeff [Alguire, playing Claudius] added that small hand gesture to shut her out, I couldn't help but watch Gertrude even as Claudius and Laertes were talking their stuff out. That little gesture seemed to me at least to totally animate Gertrude's silence and stillness – and suddenly that whole can of worms from the previous scene we'd worked on took a discernible shape. All of the stuff we'd talked about for the earlier scene I could now 'see' in her as she watched Claudius shut her out. That's going to be a great set-up for her to come back to when she brings news of Ophelia's death. I know there are a lot of words that need to be dealt with. But it's also great to see some speaking, animated stillness that keeps a character's story going when someone else might have all the lines.

<u>15 August. What a Piece of Work Is Man</u>
Great joys in the strong choices explored in last night's work. Confident rhythms and clear arguments are taking hold of 'O that this too too solid flesh' and 'O what a rogue and peasant slave.' Playing *The Mousetrap* in a dislocatingly hyper-realistic mode, on lavalier mics, like The Wooster Group doing a Lifetime TV special. And Hamlet getting Rosencrantz and Guildenstern to just stand there and look up, while he took a seat in the audience and asked us to have a gander at these two fine specimens. Heads in the clouds, clueless and needy dreamers both, infinite in faculty and destined to make the wrong choices and to be endlessly disappointing. Like Hamlet was looking into the future. His future. What a piece of work indeed.

When I look back at these blog entries, I can see a few things that weren't apparent at the time. One is the naivety of thinking that I wasn't directing, or being perceived as the director, in all this. Apart from the stage managers, and an occasional visit from another person available for text coaching, I was the only one in the room who didn't have lines. Who is the director? The director is the one who looks! Another is how much the act of writing about rehearsing processes the events of a rehearsal into something more structured, more coherent, more on point than the looser, funnier, more frustrating and more free-ranging couple of hours in the room. The blogs aren't dishonest, but they are *responding* to the work we did, even if almost immediately, in a way that is different from *working* in the moment. Again, it's not dishonest: apart from deciding the bits we're going to be looking at, I don't plan anything as a director anyway, and so the only time I can possibly know what rehearsals are about is after we have them.

Knowing what I know now about where the production went after I left, I can also see that so much of this free and open play – get it up and on its feet and try things out! – gravitated towards psychological realism. You can run the scenes right away, but you can't necessarily hide from 'why is my character doing this?' Working physically – on your feet to try out physical narratives at the same time as finding your way through the language – led to some interesting discoveries in the moment, but it also met with some resistance and distrust. What I perceived of as 'finding our way' through the Viewpoints – playing with spatial relations, developing and repeating gestural vocabulary, experimenting with variations in floor patterns and tempo and physical tension – may have seemed like (or, for those who didn't like putting it up without any table work, instilled a desire for) blocking. Not everyone can make a character discovery physically, and then just abandon that outward form while keeping the spark of forward progress alive to take into a completely different container of choreography, business and blocking in another context, with another director.

This was also nothing like an Original Practices kind of experimental process and, again, how could it have been? This wasn't a show finding its way without a director – it was a show with two directors. I was there observing, guiding and feeding back into the actors' work for every moment of those two weeks, and after those two weeks they had a very strong and experienced but different director taking them through to opening. What was it that my friend inherited upon his return? The transition was not quite the smooth baton pass we may have imagined – when I asked Jaybird how rehearsals were going (just after I got back to Pennsylvania) he joked (darkly) that the goslings had imprinted a bit on the first director they saw. I know he had been hoping for the actors to be hitting their stride, but I wonder if what he got were actors hitting *my* stride – or at least a stride where things that were 'working' were working for/with me, which would of course not necessarily be things that would work for the 'real' director or with new ideas and circumstances moving forward.

From what I could gather, the show wasn't exactly coming together. Then, a few days before opening, they lost their venue – long story, but the company found themselves in an untenable position and no good solution seemed to be forthcoming. Any of the production elements (use of that large open space for striking intimacy in the vastness, a grand entrance for the Ghost, the preshow karaoke, epic rope light paths) that had been planned or imagined or at least possible were out. It was, from what I heard, not the greatest home, but it was home. The show was almost cancelled, but at a Tuesday meeting before the planned Thursday opening, the company agreed to live or die by each other and go forward with a few words by Shakespeare and a couple of flashlights. They moved temporarily into a local park, were not entirely honest about permits when the police stopped by in the middle of the last dress rehearsal, and somehow got through the opening weekend.

What was there at the end was what was intended at the beginning: this group of people in a minimalist version of the play. But getting there was also an exercise in the unintentional stripping down of the work, not just a distillation but an often painful unbalancing act of excising the legs the thing was attempting to stand on. I went back to see the production in the second weekend of its run, when they were performing on the grounds of a farm in Efland, about half an hour west of Durham (for the third and final week they were in a high school parking lot in Chapel Hill). It was a strange experience. I suppose I still had ghost images and ideas in my head from the work we had done in the first two weeks, and probably some hazy projections of where I thought that work might have gone. I didn't really see any of that past or imagined future work. That's probably as it should have been: they had, of course, moved on. But what I felt unclear about was what exactly had taken the place of that work. To say I didn't care for it doesn't get to the heart of a complicated situation. I knew the stripped-down production had been stripped down again – stripped down from the tentative directions they were going towards with me, stripped down from all production concepts (the provocative adoption ideas seemed to figure not at all in anything playable), stripped down and taken out of the physical space it had been imagined for and rehearsed in, and stripped of its production elements (in terms of the technical bells and whistles we have come to expect even in Chamber Shakespeare). There they were, in front of a small outbuilding, in street clothes with no discernable design (I learned later that some of the actors wore different clothes to every performance), lit by a couple of flashlights held by the stage managers, making their way through the play scene by scene. What I got, or what I felt I was seeing, was the experience of a group of people coping.

Perhaps there is a difference between minimalist by intent and minimalist by necessity, arrived at through circumstances beyond everyone's – including the director's – initial understanding or control. By the same token, though: *what is a production besides 'coping' – the individual and collective responses to how things went down*? Hamlet is *Hamlet*; it was before and will be after this production. Context and contingency is the thing, and the readiness to deal with it is all. If both Jaybird and I were somewhat ambivalent about where the show ended up, perhaps that is an inevitable part of being at a director's remove from those who were just trying to cope, with new obstructions in trying circumstances, and ultimately did so. Perhaps it also measures something of a director's difficulty in coping with unfulfilled intuition, and with the vestiges of a formless hunch that didn't come off, or at least assume any recognizable relation to the form such a hunch even conceivably might have taken. Like someone driving and arguing with their GPS, I guess I just would have taken another road. But: audiences seemed to love the show, and the production got some of the strongest reviews the company had ever received.

I wonder if *hmlt* was a hit with critics and audiences because, in its constant possibility of failure, its stark and maybe startling openness, it had some new and different energy that they responded to. Maybe this is what it is *really* like when a show isn't under the tight reins of a director's control, and all the aspects of the well-made production are left at the side of the unfamiliar road this show ended up going down. Failure can also be productive – the rehearsal process is predicated on roads-not-gone-down. Perhaps it even got a bit more like Original Practices in spite of my contributions. As one of the actors explained to me later:

> We couldn't really get comfortable (in the bad sense of that word) so that meant we never really had the chance to be lazy or phoned-in, by necessity the show kept changing, and I think that may have given the show an edginess that it wouldn't have had otherwise.

Like Carroll's actors with The Factory, the LGP actors could not ignore but had to play the mighty obstructions that came their way. Ironically, the whole point of the Viewpoints work was lost, not on the actors, but on me: I was there looking out for a production, while the actors were looking out for each other. This is first principles stuff from the Viewpoints work:

it is the quality of your attention that matters most. That is how you cope. The same actor also said that 'when your venue, entrances, exits, blocking, etc., are all malleable, you find out how much you rely on each other and how aware you have to be about everything'. In the end, the show was intensely task-orientated and devised on the fly as the actors – with their own personal logic, intensely present and imitating nothing – worked just to get through it. Perhaps my blogging as the not-director was just a trap I set for myself: less writing about directing than a cautionary tale about the distinctions between theory and practice, philosophy and being. There I was, imagining obstacles and obstructions in a fiction, in a dream of passion, whereas the actors moved on to find their motives and cues in the all-too-tangible challenges of the moment.

Unless, that is, I think of directing in a very different way. Directing may not be so much authoring the show as it is facilitating focused play for the development of coping skills – and I had a hand in that, even if none of my 'ideas' showed up in the version-of-the-moment that I saw. Like Carroll's work with The Factory – which I read about well *after* this production – everything got thrown away and the work only progressed on subterranean levels. For some of the *hmlt* actors, coping with what went down was empowering and an exhilarating test of their courage and commitment to working without a safety net and with nothing to hide behind – 'true punk rock, just get out there and do it' as one put it. For another actor it was a rush, albeit a strange one:

> I have no idea what we had as we went into show-mode: we were running on pure heart and sweat and good intentions; we did what we had to do because there was no other option; we relied entirely on the language and each other; and we put what we had out into the world.

For some, 'coping' was the term used to cover the disappointment, frustration, embarrassment and even anger in letting go of what they thought they had and hoped they would be doing. One actor told me that with all the coping she felt like she'd completely forgotten how to play. Again, like the work by The Factory in the previous chapter, and like the philosophy I was espousing if not always understanding in my blog, it's turning coping *into* play that seems the crucial step. The actor who seemed the happiest about *hmlt* told me that it was embracing the unexpected that made the work incredibly inclusive for the company and its audiences. Except, perhaps, for me, sitting there puzzling over the process and not enjoying the performance. Maybe a director can never really be an actual audience member once a show has opened. As I watched good actors go down swinging

I knew there was a directing lesson in there somewhere, and that the rest of my Year of Shakespeare would give me some further opportunity to figure out what that lesson was.

**Improvised Shakespeare:** The Improvised Shakespeare Company is a Chicago group with Shakespeare in their name but who never do any Shakespeare. Instead, 'Based on one audience suggestion The Improvised Shakespeare Co. creates a fully improvised play in Elizabethan style' (improvisedshakespeare.com). When I had them to Bradford in September 2014 the show we got was *The Dancing Dryads of Denmark*, a decidedly shaggy-dog story of shape-shifting wood nymphs, misbegotten lovers and casual slaughters. I found myself thinking it was a bit more Beaumont and Fletcher than Shakespeare, but it was hilarious and a very enjoyable evening at the theatre.

Unlike an adaptation that may jettison the language and the plot but keep the characters, or a foreign film that may change the language and the characters but keep something of the story, here we were without the words, the plot, the story, the characters ... The Improvised Shakespeare Company website says that 'each of the players has brushed up on his "thee's" and "thou's" to bring you an evening of off-the-cuff comedy using the language and themes of William Shakespeare.' But are 'thee' and 'thou' really the most Shakespearean of his many, many words? What is a Shakespearean theme, exactly? Lovers are crossed? Passions are raised? People die? What the Improvised Shakespeare Company do, brilliantly, is pursue that particular night's improvised lunacy while making it sound the way most people think Shakespeare kind of sounds. This is a noble and pleasing pursuit, not without difficulties and not without enormous comedic rewards. But my job as a director is the exact opposite. While improvising new contexts and actions for Shakespeare's words, I'm trying to make Shakespeare sound kind of like my actors, to make it sound like something they could actually say. This is not about rendering Shakespeare in some instantly recognizable pop-culture cadence. But I can't, nor should I, make my actors sound 'Shakespearean'. What I can do is help make Shakespeare work for, make his words suit, the actor in the room, the one who is valiantly trying to make his or her way through the action of the play – and that was precisely what was put to the test in my next ShakesYear project.

**Suit the Word to the Action, The Action to the Word, or, Shakespeare Meant to Write 'THERE'S A FUCKING FLOATING FIRE!':** Having watched talented professional actors struggle mightily that summer to get anywhere in *hmlt* – a performance-without-a-production – I was going to make sure that the very inexperienced student actors in *A Midsummer Night's Dream* would have a solid production to shore them up, or at least to fall back on. Advance cutting made sure the run time wouldn't go over two hours even with the intermission (less experience, to me, almost always means less stamina in just getting through a show). The playing space was intimate and set up in the round (keep everyone close together so actors don't need to push their performance, keep the audience intimate so it almost can't help but feel like they are into it and on the actors' side). I worked up the perfect soundtrack (the all-Led Zeppelin was carefully chosen to maximize energy and laughter – Bottom exiting to Titania's bower to the opening of 'Dazed and Confused' will never be topped). And my scenic design (audiences entered the black box along a path through a dense thicket of Spanish moss-covered trees to an open green space over which a huge Spanish moss-covered tree arched) was, I shudder somewhat to say, really pretty. Excepting a couple of experienced actors brought in for Titania and Oberon, I was working with a very novice crew, and those elements certainly seemed helpful. I am open to the possibility that those things were also there to help me. Perhaps I am a 'good' director, but perhaps I also have acquired an acute sense of the things that I know will 'work' in order to cover my own fear of failure of the most prosaic kind. However challenging the material, I've learned always to cook it with some sugar.

From an acting standpoint, I made sure, as I always had in the past, that the cast were paraphrasing all their lines to make sure they knew exactly what they were saying at all times. I'm almost embarrassed to say that I'd never really checked that students did their paraphrases, or on the quality/accuracy of the paraphrasing they did. More importantly, I had never questioned the need or the efficacy of this device as a rehearsal tool, whether I stringently followed up on it or not. But for this show I learned a huge lesson about this time-honoured technique that I had never bothered to consider before when reflexively pulling it out of my director's bag of tricks.

One of my actors was really struggling, both to get her lines into her head and to make anything like sense out of the ones that she did know. We spent a lot of time going back and forth over her paraphrasing, which she had written out completely and thoroughly in the margins beside her lines. We tweaked some of the paraphrasing with different words that ostensibly made 'better' sense for her. We tried to identify which were her most important words (the 'hot' words, the operative terms) so she had something to aim for phrase by phrase, line by line, or image by image. By the end of each rehearsal, though, and in spite of my reassuring pep talks to send her out the door, I was aware that we were making little headway. I was a bit surprised, and a bit worried. This was a smart, motivated student. She had done her homework – the paraphrasing homework I assured her would help. Why wasn't it working?

*My Year of Shakespeare* 125

Around the same time, another actor – also struggling, also keen to 'get it right' and do it well – just came out and said: 'Can you tell me how this should sound?' One of the clichés of bad directing – and I don't know where we get this from, but I think all directors have it in our heads somewhere – is about giving line readings: 'Just say it like this...'. It probably has something to do with what Stanislavski called 'preserving the freedom of the creative artist' (Stanislavski 2010, 73), perhaps especially important for student actors, and about encouraging them to find their own way, explore their own instincts and exercise their own voice, etc. But for this production a cliché of 'bad' directing collided with my unexamined trust in the 'good' technique of paraphrasing Shakespeare to reveal something new, at least to me.

My students didn't want or need or benefit from an alternate paraphrased version of their lines. On top of the Shakespeare that they didn't understand, they then just had another batch of words, less interesting ones, that they also didn't really understand or know what to do with. In fact, some of the actors started speaking their paraphrases – after a couple of rehearsals doing that, I had to remind them that we weren't replacing Shakespeare's lines with the paraphrases but just using them to make sure they understood Shakespeare's lines, the lines they were still supposed to be saying. I should have realized much earlier that I wasn't helping them. They were just replacing words they would never say with some other words they would never say. It was the third or fourth time struggling with that very smart student who had done her paraphrasing homework – excellently – and then done it again and again that I finally realized something. They didn't need the *content* to be paraphrased – they needed a paraphrase of the *intent*. The words weren't really the problem – at least, not a problem that more words, roughly equivalent but usually less interesting, were going to fix. What they needed was some palpable, visceral sense of what was going on. And here the grain of truth in the directorially dreaded line reading was exactly the kind of life raft they were seeking – they wanted to know what the exchanges sounded like so they would have something to *play*, something to *do* with their words.

From this point we never got bogged down in vocabulary issues again. Every rehearsal was about finding the strongest intent that their lines could push forward. I never actually gave any of them a line reading (Bad Director: 'Say it this way...'). I didn't have to, once they realized that previously awkward, impenetrable or otherwise lifeless lines could sound like (Me: 'Okay, well, try making it sound like...') 'Oh my God you're so hot!' or 'I swear to God I'm going to rip your head off!' or something equally colourful but certainly full of instantly recognizable intent. This worked for less exuberant scenes as well. The actor playing Demetrius was struggling with the explanation of his change of heart to Theseus in Act IV, Scene i. I told him to try it like it was more directed to Helena than to Theseus, that it was his way of apologizing, and that the potentially (unhelpfully) florid 'But like a sickness did I loath this food;/But, as in health, come to my natural taste,/Now I do wish it, love it, long for it,/And will for evermore be true to it' should just sound as simple as 'I was shitty to you, and I'm sorry, and now I just want to be with you'. He did, it did, and this small moment became just lovely.

We had some scheduling issues, and were often missing an actor or two during larger group scenes, especially with the mechanicals. At those times, I would usually fill in rather than getting the stage manager to do it, just for the sake of trying to keep the energy up and keep things moving. A confession – I don't usually have a script in hand or even ready to hand at rehearsals, and I also don't have a photographic memory so that I have the lines at my fingertips. What I do know is what's going on. So, at the rehearsals where I'd fill in, I would just improvise something, anything for the missing character that went with what was going on. At one rehearsal where we were doing Act III, Scene i where Puck messes with the mechanicals in the forest, I had to fill in for the missing Snout. Knowing my Puck was a smoker, I had asked him at one rehearsal to flick his lighter to freak out the mechanicals. At this particular rehearsal, he was 'invisibly' flicking his lighter all around Bottom's head as the mechanicals came in and out. Apparently filling in as Snout but not remembering the pretty simple line 'O Bottom, thou art changed. What do I see on thee?' I came out with 'Bottom ... THERE'S A FUCKING FLOATING FIRE!' Students told me that it was these ad-libs with strong intent that helped them finally understand what to do with their actual lines – not what they 'meant' in dry arms-length vocabulary terms, but more vigorously translated, like Bottom himself, in ways that spurred (and supported) strong action. In Stanislavski's terms, I was able to 'whet their appetites' and help 'lead them to discover what they need to fulfill simple physical actions' (2010, 73).

Words with intention, words in action ... through rehearsing this show I understood another truth to Frank McCourt's line in *Angela's Ashes* about how speaking Shakespeare is like having jewels in your mouth. What few people note about that lovely phrase is that he also says that of course he had no idea what the words meant. What I discovered is that for my students having jewels in their mouths is not exactly empowering. Jewels are hard. Jewels in your mouth are gonna break your teeth – and eventually your spirit. Jewels are much nicer when they are set in something. At least in this case, it was only when firmly set in intention and action that they had a chance to sparkle.

**Can You Tell Me How To Get To Sesame Street?**: Thaddeus Phillips was confident that, at the end of the day and the end of the run, his one-man-band *Henry 5 Live From Times Square* (see Chapter 4) was a solid version of *Henry V*. So too with the actresses in Little Green Pig's *Richie* (Chapter 5) – they didn't particularly feel a difference between their play and Shakespeare's. Both those shows reimagined Shakespeare into very specific new (and very topical/contemporary) contexts, but both 'scripts' of these events (even though they were events you really needed to be a part of to understand anything of how they worked) were almost entirely of lines by Shakespeare. Perhaps the question of whether they were adapted or directed is easy enough to blur. I would argue, though, that even the Rude Mechs' *Fixing King John* – which has zero lines written by Shakespeare and so obviously 'fixed' with writer's tools rather than director's tools – is still *King John*, and that Stratford, Ontario outwardly-Original-Practices/inwardly-improvised production just proved the point for me: ostensibly so different, and without a single line in common, the experience felt like, they hit me like, the exact same play. So when I thought I would see what I might learn about directing Shakespeare from moving really far away from the cheerful tyranny and/or infinite openness of his texts, I chose something that I knew no one could call a 'version' of the origin play, and that – surely – could only be seen as a completely new work in its own right.

Young Jean Lee's *LEAR* is certainly a wild ride. Lee is one of the most fearless and fascinating theatre-makers working today – I think *The Shipment* is one of the essential pieces of twenty-first century American theatre thus far. In the spirit of devised work, Lee sets herself a task for the creation of each show, and that is to do a show she doesn't know how to do and probably shouldn't be doing. She tends to move the theatre away from its seeming home port of traditional dramatic structure/realism of presentation into deeper, choppier waters – her Black identity politics piece *The Shipment* is half deadpan minstrel show, half comedy of bad manners that gets blown up in its final two lines, while *Untitled Feminist Show* is a movement piece performed by six physically diverse actresses both without words and without clothes. The script for *LEAR* spends about two-thirds of its time with *King Lear*'s younger generation – Goneril, Regan, Cordelia, Edmund and Edgar – being horrible to each other and to themselves as a way of avoiding dealing with how they have been horrible to their fathers, before veering into a verbatim sequence from a classic episode of the American television series *Sesame Street* dealing with the death of longstanding character Mr. Hooper, before veering again into a devastating monologue of a young man trying to process and/or fight against his emotional detachment from his ageing father. Again, in the mode of devised work, *LEAR* is asking a particularly potent question about both an old story and contemporary life: so, in the face of the death of the older generation, how are the kids holding up? The answers it generates are diverse and provocative.

And yet – some of the critics at *LEAR*'s first production (which was also directed by Lee, in New York in 2010) asked a rather singular question of this piece, this completely new piece of writing that had almost no lines by Shakespeare in it: *what does it tell us about Shakespeare's play?* It is, one imagines, the same question they would ask when seeing a production of Shakespeare's actual play. Is this the black hole of Bardolatry sucking everything into its gaping maw? Perhaps, but it is also the long shadow of the traditional drama critic's belief that performances of plays are about things that can be articulated in the same dramatic/thematic/interpretive/ character-driven/psychological-realist mode as ever ... and where a production of Young Jean Lee's audacious experiment gets read not quite in its own right but against the script – *another* script, not its own, and apparently one not even in the back but still in the forefront of the critic's mind. Some of *LEAR*'s critics couldn't see the question, and the structure used to engage with the question, because they were hooked on and went down with the Shakespearean anchor. For them, it seems, everything has to be (understood as) an interpretation, and nothing can just be its own experience.

The production I directed (in Bradford in 2015 at the end of my Shakes-Year experiment) had the advantage of audiences that didn't know much, if anything, about Shakespeare's play, and so were inadvertently taking Lee's work much more at face value. I heard back both in my classes and from the actors in the show that there were those in the Bradford audiences who hated it: 'it was just weird and stupid' is as good a summary as any. There were those who, more benignly, felt they didn't get it: 'I don't understand why we suddenly went to Sesame Street, and then who was the guy at the end?' sums up that camp. Finally, there were those for whom something *happened*. My favourite story was of a student whose girlfriend left the theatre in silence, went out for drinks and food with some friends afterwards, and an hour later started crying and saying that she needed to stay in better touch with her family.

The brilliance of that audience member's response, however, makes it easier for me to dodge a small detail about the process of making this production. As a director, I have long since stopped putting director's notes in my programmes and I no longer start rehearsals by explaining the play, but I partly figured my way through *LEAR* by assuring my cast, 'This play is weird but, really, it makes a pretty good case that *King Lear* is about...'. Aha!

What was this? Textual interpretation, once-removed? My version of *King Lear*, twice-removed? Was I in fact thinking just like those New York critics who only saw Lee's work in terms of Shakespeare's work? Was I really directing in the most traditional way, with this most experimental or postmodern take on Shakespeare? Perhaps on the most pragmatic level I *had* to say something of what the play was 'about' so I could convince a whole bunch of confused students, in both my performance and my stagecraft practicums, that the endeavour wasn't fruitless. So yes, I told them the play was about how the kids are coping. Then I caught myself, and rephrased it as our guiding *question*: so, how are the kids holding up? Our *anchor* was the loss of parents or parental figures (in *King Lear*, in *Sesame Street*, in our lives). Our *structure* was a conscious and gleeful blowing up of anything like traditional narrative propriety – Lee handed us some grenades and we had to figure out when, where and how far to throw them. We did some table work, about the question and the anchor. There was some attention paid to psychology and emotional states and how it might 'make sense' that characters/people might act in this way. We talked a lot about families. I talked a lot about my dad. Major ideas and themes were explicated and pursued and framed rather coherently ... for a time. And then, like it always does, the practical work of making theatre became more about the in-the-moment decisions concerning action, about setting tasks within the structure to throw that action into sharper relief, about how to maximize the theatrical interest and pleasure of the experience, and about how to ask the question better. So in our production speeches were overlapped, the actress playing Cordelia asked for and got amplification and a sweet mic drop to mark a major transition, snippets of old home movies flashed on a screen that an actor mimicked on stage, a slowed-down and soul-shredding cover of The Pixies' 'Where Is My Mind' scored an extended final movement sequence, etc. Nothing will come of nothing, and the play (Shakespeare's, Lee's) doesn't speak for itself – we had to devise the action, to embody these words, and to take a point of view as storytellers and artists. We had to make things harder, and simpler, recognizable from a couple of angles and unpredictable from all the others. And that is directing for me, Shakespearean or otherwise.

# Part III
Provocation and Debate

# 8
# A Conversation with Rude Mechs

Rude Mechs is an ensemble-based theatre collective from Austin, Texas. Here's how the company describes itself:

> Since 1995, Rude Mechs has created a mercurial slate of original theatrical productions that represent a genre-averse cocktail of big ideas, cheap laughs, and dizzying spectacle. What these works hold in common are the use of play to make performance, the use of theaters as meeting places for audiences and artists, and the use of humor as a tool for intellectual investigation.
>
> (rudemechs.com/aboutus)

I asked the co-producing artistic directorship (COPAD) to have a conversation with me about directing and Shakespeare today. Here's how the artistic directorship describe themselves:

> The artistic directors of Rude Mechs often compare ourselves to a cycling team because of the fluid manner with which we switch roles – when one of us is having a hard time another swoops in to take the lead. We often compare the full company to a band because of the various harmonies you get when you combine the talents of the individual members and their particular training, histories, and experiences. But perhaps the most astonishing description is the one that lacks all metaphorical drapery – Rude Mechanicals is made up of six artistic directors who have chosen, day after day, to commit to each other for 15 years. As a company of almost 30 actors, designers, and crew we apprentice ourselves to the idea that the

best work is made by combining the depth of multiple points of view with the discipline to speak as a single voice.

(rudemechs.com/aboutus)

Four of the COPADs – Kirk Lynn, Shawn Sides, Madge Darlington and Lana Lesley – as well as Managing Director Alexandra Bassett, chatted with me over email for a week in July 2017. Here is our conversation. I conducted it in much the same way as I direct: find some good people, ask some questions, get out of the way, curate what comes in.

*KEVIN EWERT: What does directing look like to you?*

KIRK LYNN: I am a writer. I have almost no interest in the actual world. Or to be a little sharper, I take the actual world and turn it into fiction. I think directors take fiction and turn it into the actual world.

I like to conceive. Once I understand how a project works, how a narrative will end, I have trouble completing it.

So the director looks like this remarkably grounded person. She is a conceiver, like a writer, but also a realist. I think if the director has a fault it is likely abandoning things that can't be done. And the director looks very much like Shawn Sides, and a little like Madge, and a little like Alex. And then there are some bits and pieces of Melanie Joseph (Foundry Theatre) and Annie Kauffman (The Civilians) and Katie Pearl (PearlDamour) and Courtney Sale (Seattle Children's Theatre) and Luke Leonard (Monk Parrots). I have been very lucky in that I make most of my work with Shawn Sides and then most of the rest of it with Madge and Alex and then that means that most of my work is with the Rude Mechs and we know how to work with one another.

But you didn't ask what the director looks like, you asked with the act of directing looks like. So let me get a little provocation going. I think directing is the act of keeping one's possibilities open for as long as possible. 'We might do this or this. We might set it in the ocean but we might set it in a hotel.' It costs the director nothing to imagine two different settings, but the writer or the designer has to make two separate drafts. Directing is a live act that requires other people. Writing is a contemplative act that requires silence and loneliness and secrecy. A lot of people laugh when I say 'I have some typing to do,' instead of writing... But I don't necessarily think writing is a live act. By the time you are typing you may have already done all the writing in your head and dreaming and running and praying. I don't see that side of directing... or maybe it's just the inverse, there's some of it, like there's some writing while you're typing. But most of the directing I see is live in the room.

I think directing is also more dangerous and more embarrassing. Most of my most awful drafts never get seen. When I have to yell at myself or the text or the characters or the computer or the printer, no one has to see that. But directors get caught failing and getting frustrated and losing their cooooools.

LANA LESLEY: Watching directing looks like watching someone run at full speed with a very fragile egg in their jaws. It looks like someone who stayed up all night staring at a set model and pushing dolls around to make sure there was something to do when everyone is just sitting there STARING at you. It looks like someone trying to reassemble an onion. It looks like someone squat-lifting someone else every night from 7pm to 11pm.

Directing without a love for it (which is all I have personally experienced) looks like having to schedule art-making around an ever-changing and ever-growing list of conflicts. It looks like a bunch of people that *want* you to lead but don't want you to not let them lead the moment they have an idea.

I've directed two giant-ass pieces for Rude Mechs – one with 14 people, one with 21 people. I was my own playwright on one of them and I fought with my own damn self over my really clear vision and my really important text. And I fought with myself hard when one of us would say the play 'wanted' something and the other of us would say it 'wanted' something else entirely. Who the fuck cares what the play wants?

SHAWN SIDES: Directing looks like marshalling the forces in the room against the tyranny of 'being original', inviting some stuff, offering some stuff, coaxing out the aesthetic – or just spotting it hiding behind something and pointing towards it, being the outside-eye-in-chief, tending the flame, dancing around personalities, building structure out of beautiful chaos and then tearing it down and using the pieces to try a different structure, if there's bad news – being the bearer. Directing is as lonely as writing, just not as solitary. There's a lot of writing involved. A lot of in-your-head work. You just can't actually draft anything without other people. Or, like, do some directing exercises at home every day to keep up your practice. But it's not all in the room any more than acting is. Directing is completely unnecessary. Actors are necessary. Actors who hate improvising make writers necessary. Directors are just around if you want us. But then if you do invite us in we take up a lot of room. I think a lot of folks, especially in the devising community, are shifting to a general 'theatre-maker' title so as not to get pigeonholed and also to be able to shake off all the preconceived ideas of clearly defined roles that separate writing vs acting vs directing vs choreography vs dramaturgy vs design, not to mention vs producing vs marketing vs stage management.

ALEXANDRA BASSETT: Directing looks like listening. Full body sensorial listening. And also like the pure delight and disgust of a baby. 'YES do it again! YES! This time with the shoulder!! YES AAH YES!!'

Usually I'm working with playwrights that are still tinkering in or overhauling their plays, actors that are memorizing lines and trying movements, designers who haven't received confirmation of the theatre yet, lyrics that haven't been put to melody yet, only this much budget, etc. etc., so the logic of the project at hand feels like a stellar nursery nebula.

All of us in the room, we try things out, asking questions, tuning and testing our perceptions, checking in-checking in, blasting this part up to the rafters just to see, or that part we all thought was rafter-worthy – putting it in a small quiet room, and again checking in-checking in ... til that checking in hones the play rehearsal nebula into the pulsing constellation of the performance.

It also can look like a momentary epic nadir dark cold fear in the soul. Fidgeting and thinking, how? But why, how? Lots of giggling and long talks staring forward into empty space with different textures and glows. Lots of gripping middle-of-the-night ideas and a voice recorder. A lot of purposeful vulnerability and resilience.

Directing is associative and intuitive, working to sense what provokes what. Directing is also so awfully logical and full of logistics. When the logic and logistics crystallize together by the end of the process, they sound like dream poems to me: 'Reach for the invisible orange, it's the memory, swoosh your body, she flies in, fabric gusts from the right, she turns around, cicada sounds, we're then now.'

Directing looks like structuring energy.

## *KEVIN EWERT: What does directing Shakespeare look like?*

KIRK LYNN: You know, most of the squares they get to come through University of Texas at Austin [where Lynn is Associate Professor in the Department of Theatre and Dance], it looks like a facsimile of a copy of a misunderstanding of a stereotype that was based on a flawed method that was outdated twenty years ago. You think by the sheer power of all that idiocy they would stumble on something as awful and new as punk rock. But instead it's like the greeting card industry. 90 per cent of *King Lears* can't be differentiated. They say 'happy birthday.'

I can't understand why more actors don't rebel. Meet in secret in their apartments and stage nude versions. Or store up all the boredom they get fed in rehearsal and then once the paying customers show up, scream all their lines at the top of their voices.

There's a great section in your book where you talk about an Original Practices nutter. But what made me swoon was that this director doesn't know what his play is going to look like. He doesn't walk in with a line he's going to feed the actors in order to convince them to feed the audience. 'This play is about how old people should die sooner.' He comes into the rehearsal room to play.

Most of the Rude Mechs met at a programme called Shakespeare at Winedale and the idea of actually playing was so important. But, of course, all ideas can be taught to eat themselves. At Winedale the idea of play had to be so pure that you couldn't play with an interpretation, for instance that *Taming of the Shrew* was sexist, or that *Hamlet* could be viewed as a political thriller... Still, my point is that *playing* was the most superior quality.

SHAWN SIDES: I don't think directing Shakespeare is any different than directing any other well-known text. There is a point, well before the point of public domain, when a play can become so well known that it is part of received culture and at that point the historical information becomes another layer of meaning, whether you like it or not. And by default, what the performing company is 'doing with' that information becomes a thing that will be paid attention to. (You already sum this up very well in your Intro.) There's an extra freedom for directors in working with a well-known text. When you're working with a brand new play and audiences don't have a preconceived notion of what's going to 'happen' that you can play with or play to or pee on or whatever – it's a different kind of rhythm and a different kind of attention.

LANA LESLEY: Directing Shakespeare is like time travel to a time I wouldn't want to be alive.

ALEXANDRA BASSETT: I'm gonna say all that I said above, but the playwright's dead. So I'd be carrying around those two volumes of the Alexander Schmidt Shakespeare Lexicon and Quotation Dictionary. I'd consult RSC notes. I'd call John Hadden. I'd write the play by hand just to see.

More vast and regal, more people flowing in and out. All juicier with the mouth. More chances for a moon.

**KEVIN EWERT: *What about directing Shakespeare is absolutely unique, and what about it is the same as directing anything else?***

KIRK LYNN: I think the pretension is unique. I think the ignorance about contemporary literature and directing methods is unique. I think the self-satisfaction is unique. I think you give a Young Jean Lee play or an Annie Baker play or Sarah Delappe's *Wolves* to a Shakespearean director and nine out of 10 of them are lost. You ask nine out of 10 Shakespeare directors to talk to a living grown-up collaborative writer and and t-t-they don't cuz who knows to say what? But you go vice versa and take Sam Gold or Lila Neugebauer or Young Jean Lee and ask them to heat up *Two Noble Kinsmen* for you and POW SHAPOW!

I think the part that should be more like anything else is thinking about the audience, thinking about how we consume culture these days, where we wanna meet, how we wanna sing the songs we know, how we wanna dance with you and taste the wine ourselves. More *Sleep No More* and less 8th grade culture lesson.

SHAWN SIDES: I'm glad I don't know who Kirk is so mad at. My answer is just the same as my one above.

LANA LESLEY: Blah blah blah the language blah blah blah getting the meaning across blah blah blah to accent or not blah blah blah to set it in dystopian future or not blah blah blah to cross-gender cast or not ... My smarter better colleagues who bill themselves as directors should take this one.

ALEXANDRA BASSETT: I enjoy the linguistics of Shakespeare's text. The syntax is fun, the vocabulary is fun. The language is younger, so it sounds so much freer. Images are unfettered by today's overused phrasing. Thoughts move faster.

Yeah, Kirk, I think the acting training around Shakespeare often comes off like pretension too. Not the training's fault, though. When I was acting, I worked with a bunch of Shakespeare & Company members and had a couple teachers from the RSC. Some of the Shakes and Co guys followed the Linklater method: they would examine their breath, vowels, consonants, and sound placement in the body. Some planted distinct thoughts on top of lines like flags. The RSC teachers stressed that following Shakespeare's punctuation is the best route to true expression: 'a colon marks a new related thought: like a springboard the thought jumps off: new thought!' Have a new thought, use a new register...

All this training can be incredibly useful, freeing even! But so often classical plays I end up seeing now just look and sound like training. Behold the resonant voices, the array of status postures. It can be hollow and calculated. That is such a disappointment at a show. I want any play to feel its own version of fresh and original, electric and connected.

*KEVIN EWERT: How has devising and company-created work changed the way you look at making productions out of existing scripts? Anything specific to that regarding classical texts, or to Shakespeare?*

KIRK LYNN: I think the premise of this question is a load of shit. All work is devised. Shakespeare is the most devised shit you can find! Some dude digging around in Holinshed's Chronicles for plots and cribbing scenes from Marlowe that then get reworked by actors and publishers and liars, that they get handed off to college dropouts who wanna set the whole thing in a misconception of what life was authentically like in the 1600s. That's the secret to devising. Act like you're totally never gonna do it. You have to lie to yourself something serious to believe there is a difference between Shakespeare and whatever you mean by devised work. We barely know any of the actual text Shakespeare actually wrote, all we have is folios and they're so different from what we perform. We don't have any original copies, but why not assume those are as different as the folios from the Arden editions.

Besides this thought: I don't listen to Top 40 radio. I like the indie shit. How do I get ahold of the Elizabethan plays that only played one night and were too weird and wild but inspired Shakespeare the way that Big Freedia inspired Beyonce?

SHAWN SIDES: Hm, well, I don't think you were trying to imply that Shakespeare didn't devise. I think you were just saying those scripts exist and I think you're asking something about interpreting versus generating. I get really lost in Kirk's logic but I think his point is good if I am interpreting (which is not devising) it correctly: devising → interpreting is a spectrum not a binary. Is that it? I'm not sure. I'm afraid this is a semantics game and I'm getting sucked in.

ALEXANDRA BASSETT: Oh shucks, each project is its own unique conundrum!

MADGE DARLINGTON: I'm in the UK right now with my family. I've gotten to see five Shakespeare plays in the last two weeks. *Antony and Cleopatra* by the RSC in Stratford, *Much Ado* and *Twelfth Night* at Shakespeare's Globe in London, and *Love's Labour's Lost* and *Midsummer* by different companies in Oxford. I've been lucky enough to spend six summer seasons in the UK through my own or my spouse's work.

I can say that the trend this season is metaphorizing the text. Yes, companies have been placing Shakespeare's plays in different settings for ages but often in these productions the text stays sacrosanct while the production's unique take on the play manifests solely in costume, set, and sound design. This season, to both good and ill effect, the text be damned. Whole speeches, even well-known speeches were cut or edited to reflect the play's setting. *Love's Labour's* tossed the Pageant of the Nine Worthies (the play-within-the-play in the final scene) in favour of *HMS Pinafore*. As the play was set in early twentieth-century Oxford, it was a clever substitution, but in my opinion, did nothing to enhance the performance. It seemed like change for change's sake.

Creation Theatre in Oxford was on trend in the experimental theatre world by turning *Midsummer* into a promenade play. The audience was split into groups of people meeting at different pubs, given flowers to wear that identified us as members of Hippolyta's or Theseus's wedding parties, then sent on a journey with clues around the train station area of Oxford where we encountered different characters in their plight. Highlights for me were being shoved into a cramped van, as though being kidnapped by Frances Flute, and having to walk into a Dosa restaurant to pick up 'take out' for Puck that turned out to be a walkie talkie wrapped in foil that delivered my group's next clue. Creation also reduced the 'rude mechanicals' to three players...Quince, Bottom, and Flute who were such a good comedy team that I didn't miss the other rudes or the original text one bit.

The most successful example of messing with the text, by far, was Emma Rice's direction of *Twelfth Night* at the Globe. Emma Rice was hired as the first female artistic director of the Globe in early 2016. The board of Shakespeare's Globe has already ousted her for failing to adhere to original practices. They are so offended by her use of mic'd actors and stage lights that they are blind to her directing genius and to the audience's delight. The *Twelfth Night* I saw was joyful and celebratory, as it should be. How brilliant to have Feste the jester (and singer) played by a drag queen. Suddenly Feste's mournful side made sense to me. Feste was ever present, a part of the ensemble, but also aloof, the way society's critics often are. But it is not simply that Feste was played by a drag queen (change for change's sake) but the way Feste's text was divided, giving the philosophical arguments between Feste and Olivia to Fabian, one of Olivia's servants, and letting Feste hold the place of singer, Chorus, and Muse. There was reverence to the text in the production, and also irreverence which performs exactly the Saturnalian, topsy-turvy celebration that Twelfth Night is. This play succeeded on so many levels that others do not. The characters were distinct but all of the same world. The ensemble is emphasized in the transitions, where actors with lead roles dropped character to become part of the dance team. To me that's vital for a Shakespeare play, a strong sense of ensemble.

Josette Simon is exquisite as Cleopatra in the RSC's *Antony and Cleopatra* but the rest of the actors seemed on their own acting island. The play was not of a piece. The actor playing Enobarbus has earned praise as Julius Caesar, in the 'Roman Season' in rep at the RSC presently, but as Enobarbus, his acting style was so different from others that he seemed to be in another play.

Kirk's *Fixing* plays appealed to me because of the way he is both reverent and irreverent with the text. The cussing and modern vernacular express, in contemporary, relatable terms, what the characters are feeling. I approached directing *Fixing King John* as I've approached directing other 'straight' Shakespeare plays. I like to question the feel of the world and of the room. I like to try to create a sense of ensemble. I pay attention to the rhetorical intent of each scene and strive to stay true to it. I pay attention to status of characters and when the status changes through action or text. I encourage actors to not collapse the stage, but open out to the audience. And I make sure we serve beer and wine during the play.

*KEVIN EWERT: Any other thoughts?*

KIRK LYNN: At the beginning of your book you note that the director has become the central figure of the modern theatre. This seems absurd on its face. Annie Baker is more well known than Sam Gold. Young Jean Lee directs but is known as a writer. There is this great transference of playwrights to television. If you can write a play you can write for TV, but being able to direct a play paves the way for almost no advancement. There are more grants for playwrights. There are more development opportunities for scripts. Regardless of the question of whether this is fair or good, this is no longer an age where the director is the central figure of the modern theatre.

SHAWN SIDES: The transference of playwrights to television is the proof of their centrality to theatre?!? True or False: If you can write a play you can write for TV. And then the best part – Kirk, I am totally gobsmacked that you have equated getting the fuck out of the squalor and ignominy of playwriting and into the bright pretty lights and glamour of TV-land as – obviously and of course we all know – 'ADVANCEMENT'. Dude. Why bother with the playwriting step?! GOBSMACKED! But you are right that directors are not the central figure of the modern theatre. Maybe in the 70s and/or 80s but not now I don't think.

KIRK LYNN: I think I'm talking less about my own values than current cultural norms. Although I do watch more TV than plays. I still read more novels than watch TV. I think the world looks at the theatre and says, 'what can I steal from here?' and mostly the world steals writers. But you can place whatever metric on it you want. We both have a gut instinct that since the 80s the centrality-spotlight has moved on from the director... I think you're likely right when you point to a new centrality around the theatre-maker... I think looking at Rachel Chavkin or Will Davis, they are going to get stolen and they are something more than a traditional director.

KEVIN EWERT: Maybe that's kind of the subtext of my book, or at least of the choices of things I wanted to have in it, including the thoughts of you folks. It can seem that the ShakesWorld is somehow different from and often far behind the broader theatre world. There is lip service paid to ensembles but it isn't company-created work in the way you or I would recognize it, and the traditional director still runs the show: it's the singular auteur as opposed to the collaborative, full-company-authored event! It may be a while yet before theatre-makers in the Rude Mechs or Pig Iron or Gob Squad or Forced Entertainment mode can move seamlessly into 'directing' for classical repertoire companies and then move back again.

KIRK LYNN: It's interesting to think about a book on directing Shakespeare when there was no director as we understand the term. It again feeds into the notion that Shakespeare has more to do with devising than almost any other practice, but we wanna pretend like it doesn't. It seems the height of silliness to be a director of Shakespeare who is into Original Practices. I love the idea of a script being 'a good problem' (p. 14). I am trying to learn to write better and better problems – like the composer of crossword puzzles or someone who lays out trails in a national park. The idea of director-as-interpreter makes it sound like someone who writes copy for an Ikea catalogue. They are engaged exclusively with the what-it-is of a thing, not the question of how it will be used in my life. The director who wants to get into the writer's head to try to understand what he wanted to say, must first study self-deception: 'can I teach myself to believe my own lies so that when I try to con myself into knowing what Shakespeare intended, I will believe myself?'

Hear! hear! to Jordan Tannahill's idea about making theatre to learn from your shortcomings (p. 28)! Making mistakes and learning from them takes time. I am still perfecting my mistake making ... soon I will be ready to move on to learning my first thing. I also love meeting the concept of 'mickey mousing' (p. 35). So much work that seeks to align the motivation with the text feels like this description. And I would love to smash the idea that there are any masterpieces. Just the phrase is awful. There's shit you like. It's no better than the shit she likes or the shit he likes. And none of it is worthy of study. Study is an action worthy in and of itself. Study of obscure work or popular work or amateur work, this isn't wasted study ... it's study that has generated enough passion to fuel an escape velocity from the gravity of masterpieces.

The description of devising that Harvie and Lavender offer (p. 39) is very much the current method of the Rude Mechs, but I wonder where is the audience in all this? Where is the director who wants to rehearse with her audience as the Rudes like to? To workshop something with the audience so we can collaborate with their ideas and opinions and boredom and drunkenness and loudness and shame and sadness and laughter!

# Annotated Reading List

### Practice: Polemics and Big Pictures Today

Jordan Tannahill. *Theatre of the Unimpressed: In Search of Vital Drama*. Toronto: Coach House Books, 2015.

Tannahill's brilliant, bracing polemic 'take[s] the pulse of contemporary English-language theatre' (13) and offers incisive critiques of the moribund and the truly adventurous and invigorating forms he encounters. This is a very personal book, and Tannahill is a wicked and witty guide, but the insights are deep and inspiring.

Howard Shalwitz. 'Theatrical Innovation: Whose Job Is It?' Address to National Conference of the Theatre Communications Guild, Boston, MA, 21 June 2012. Accessed at http://www.tcgcircle.org/2012/07/theatrical-innovation-whose-job-is-it/ on 26 January 2018.

This piece, written by the artistic director of Washington DC's Woolly Mammoth Theatre Company, has been in the back of my mind through most of the process of writing this book. Shalwitz has much to say, or, perhaps more accurately, many questions to ask, concerning contemporary American theatre practice and the assembly line of (much of) its creation. The key is in a conversation Shalwitz had with director Dominique Serrand in which Serrand told him: 'In Europe, the first job of the director is to reinvent the art form of theatre for every production. In the US, this job isn't even on the list of what most directors hope to achieve.'

### Directors

Anne Bogart. *A Director Prepares: Seven Essays on Art and Theatre*. New York: Routledge, 2001.
——. *And Then You Act: Making Art in an Unpredictable World*. New York: Routledge, 2007.
——. *What's The Story: Essays About Art, Theater and Storytelling*. New York: Routledge, 2014.

Bogart's three books are philosophical but eminently readable how-tos and why-tos for artists and theatre-makers today. As far as directing is concerned, Bogart posits three types:

1. One kind of director's talent is the force of his or her vision. In these rehearsals, actors flourish by giving over to the magnetism of the director's idea, conception, and imagination.
2. The second kind of director is able to see each individual in the room. These rehearsals are about recognizing progress on an individual basis.
3. Finally, there are directors who can recognize and are guided by the available inspiration in the room and allow the room to be lead by whoever is inspired and in the 'flow' of the moment (Bogart 2007, 59).

Bogart is the third, and the collection of anecdotes and advice in these books are encouragement for others to find the third way as well.

Peter Brook. *The Empty Space*. New York: Atheneum/Macmillan, 1968.
——. *The Shifting Point*. London: Methuen, 1988.
——. *The Open Door*. New York: Anchor Books, 2005 (originally published 1993).
——. *The Quality of Mercy: Reflections on Shakespeare*. London: Nick Hern, 2013.
Margaret Croyden. *Conversations with Peter Brook 1970–2000*. New York: Faber and Faber, 2003.

Brook is probably the towering figure of twentieth-century directing – and not just because of the sheer length of his career. Any or all of these volumes capture something of the restlessness that has marked both his encounters with Shakespeare and continuous reinventions within the art form.

Gabriella Giannachi and Mary Luckhurst, eds. *On Directing: Interviews with Directors*. New York: St. Martin's, 1999.
Shomit Mitter and Maria Shevtsova, eds. *Fifty Key Theatre Directors*. New York: Routledge, 2005.
Maria Shevtsova and Christopher Innes. *Directors/Directing: Conversations on Theatre*. Cambridge: Cambridge University Press, 2009.

Three treasure troves: *Fifty Key Theatre Directors* of scholarly appraisals of key twentieth- and twenty-first-century figures beginning with Antoine and Stanislavski; *On Directing* and *Directors/Directing* of interviews with leading contemporary practitioners.

146 *Annotated Reading List*

John Russell Brown, ed. *The Routledge Companion to Directors' Shakespeare*. New York: Routledge, 2008.

31 writers on 31 directors – from Tyrone Guthrie to Peter Hall to Deborah Warner to Julie Taymor. This substantial volume offers a reader extraordinary opportunities for cross-pollination of ideas, whether in striking similarities or radical differences over a century's worth of approaches.

## Directing and Devising

Jen Harvie and Andy Lavender, eds. *Making Contemporary Theatre: International Rehearsal Processes*. Manchester: Manchester University Press, 2010.
Duska Radosavljevic. *The Contemporary Ensemble: Interviews with Theatre-Makers*. New York: Routledge, 2013.

I spend a lot of time on these two books in the theory section – taken together they are a perfect primer to what we might think of as Post-Director's Theatre and to contemporary ideas of theatre-making.

Eugenio Barba. *On Directing and Dramaturgy: Burning the House*. New York: Routledge, 2010.

Founder of the Odin Teatret as well as the International School of Theatre Anthropology, Barba is a director and theoretician of international renown. This overview of his life's work offers a number of striking comparisons with more current theatre practitioners. He charts his arrival at the notion of performance as a *'theatrical composition resulting from a plurality of executions*: that of the actor, that of the director and that of the spectator' (13, original emphasis). Of especial note is his articulation of an actor's dramaturgy which remains independent of anything like directorial or authorial intentions, and of a spectator's dramaturgy which is co-created as an integral aspect of performance.

Anne Bogart and Tina Landau. *The Viewpoints Book: A Practical Guide to Viewpoints and Composition*. New York: Theatre Communications Group, 2005.

An excellent practical primer to methodologies of theatrical creation that are not derived from the play and what it means, or from the director and what she tells you.

## Contexts: History and Theory

Eric Bentley, ed. *The Theory of the Modern Stage*. London: Penguin, 1990 (reprint of revised 1976 edition).

Although strangely missing Strindberg's introduction to *Miss Julie*, Bentley's collection gives us many of the primary theoretical texts of the modern theatre. Of especial interest to the modern realistic director/dictator and director-as-coherence-delivery-device are things like Adolphe Appia's articulation of the director's 'principal effort' being 'to convince the individual members of his acting company that only the arduous subjection of their personalities to the unity of the production will create an important result' (in Bentley 1990, 49) and Émile Zola's insistence that plays, costumes, sets, diction, 'all must march in step' (in Bentley 1990, 369) to create the desired naturalistic effect.

Simon Shepherd. *Direction*. New York: Palgrave Macmillan, 2012.
Christopher Innes and Maria Shevtsova. *The Cambridge Introduction to Theatre Directing*. Cambridge: Cambridge University Press, 2013.
Avra Sidiropoulou. *Authoring Performance: The Director in Contemporary Theatre*. New York: Palgrave Macmillan, 2011.

All three of these books offer excellent, exhaustive overviews of the rise and evolution of the director in the modern theatre: Shepherd is especially good balancing notions of art and organization, and Sidiropoulou focuses intensely on the relationship of auteur directors and texts.

Hans-Thies Lehmann. *Postdramatic Theatre*, translated by Karen Jurs-Munby. New York: Routledge, 2006 (German edition 1999).

Lehmann gives us the theory of new theatre forms. Although decentring the Aristotelian monolith of dramatic creation, Lehmann, like Aristotle, is descriptive rather than proscriptive: the elegant theorizing came from the interesting work he was seeing, and it remains a vivid lens through which to view and better understand the mindsets and methodologies of cutting-edge practitioners today.

# Bibliography

Artaud, Antonin. *The Theatre and Its Double*, translated by Mary Caroline Richards. New York: Grove Press, 1958.
Barba, Eugenio. *On Directing and Dramaturgy: Burning the House*. New York: Routledge, 2010.
Barton, John. *Playing Shakespeare*. London: Methuen, 1984.
Bentley, Eric, ed. *The Theory of the Modern Stage*. London: Penguin, 1990 (reprint of revised 1976 edition).
Berry, Ralph. *On Directing Shakespeare*. London: Hamish Hamilton, 1989.
Billington, Michael. 'Troilus and Cressida – Review.' *The Guardian*, 9 August 2012.
——. 'The War – Art Theatre with a Vengeance.' *The Guardian*, 10 August 2014.
Boenisch, Peter and Thomas Ostermeier. *The Theatre of Thomas Ostermeier*. New York: Routledge, 2016.
Bogart, Anne. *A Director Prepares: Seven Essays on Art and Theatre*. New York: Routledge, 2001.
——. *And Then You Act: Making Art in an Unpredictable World*. New York: Routledge, 2007.
——. *What's The Story: Essays About Art, Theater and Storytelling*. New York: Routledge, 2014.
——. 'The Role of Storytelling in the Theatre of the Twenty-First Century.' Address to the 39th Humana Festival, 28 March 2015. Accessed at http://howlround.com/the-role-of-storytelling-in-the-theatre-of-the-twenty-first-century on 26 January 2018.
Bogart, Anne and Tina Landau. *The Viewpoints Book: A Practical Guide to Viewpoints and Composition*. New York: Theatre Communications Group, 2005.
Bogdanov, Michael and Michael Pennington. *The English Shakespeare Company: The Story of 'The Wars of the Roses' 1986–1989*. London: Nick Hern, 1990.
Braun, Edward. *The Director and the Stage: From Naturalism to Grotowski*. London: Methuen, 1982.
——, trans. and ed. *Meyerhold on Theatre*. Revised Edition. London: Methuen, 1991.
Brody, Richard. 'The Misplaced Nostalgia for Movies Like "The Graduate".' *The New Yorker*, 8 July 2015.
Brook, Peter. *The Empty Space*. New York: Atheneum/Macmillan, 1968.
——. *The Shifting Point*. London: Methuen, 1988.
——. *The Open Door*. New York: Anchor Books, 2005 (originally published 1993).
——. *The Quality of Mercy: Reflections on Shakespeare*. London: Nick Hern, 2013.
Brown, John Russell, ed. *The Routledge Companion to Directors' Shakespeare*. New York: Routledge, 2008.
Carroll, Tim. 'TC's Intro to Hamlet Project'. August 2006. Accessed at http://thefactory.wikifoundry.com/page/TC%27s+Intro+to+Hamlet+Project on 26 January 2018.
——. 'Notes on a Supreme Hamlet by TC'. July 2008. Accessed at http://thefactory.wikifoundry.com/page/Notes+On+a+Supreme+Hamlet+By+TC on 26 January 2018.

Clapp, Susannah. 'Shakespeare Trilogy Review – Phyllida Lloyd's Searing Triumph.' *The Guardian*, 27 November 2016.
Conlogue, Ray. 'Enlightenment or Pretension?' *The Globe and Mail*, 13 June 1988.
Cowie, Andrew. 'Is Troilus and Cressida As Bad As Everyone Says?' Bloggingshakespeare.com, 16 August 2012. Accessed at http://bloggingshakespeare.com/is-troilus-and-cressida-as-bad-as-everyone-says on 26 January 2018.
Croyden, Margaret. *Conversations with Peter Brook 1970–2000*. New York: Faber and Faber, 2003.
Darling, Michael. 'Q & A with Rude Mechanicals Playwright Kirk Lynn.' *The Texas Observer*, 22 November 2013.
Dessen, Alan. *Rescripting Shakespeare: The Text, the Director, and Modern Productions*. Cambridge: Cambridge University Press, 2002.
Dietz, Steven. 'On Directing: A Modest Proposal.' *American Theatre*, Vol. 24, No. 3, March 2007, 54.
Di Salvo, Gina M. 'The Framing of the Shrew' in *Chicago Shakespeare Theater: Suiting the Action to the Word*, edited by Regina Buccola and Peter Kanelos. DeKalb: Northern Illinois University Press, 2013.
Douthit, Lou. 'Spelunking with Shakespeare.' Howlround.com, 30 September 2015. Accessed at http://howlround.com/spelunking-with-shakespeare on 26 January 2018.
Ebert, Roger. 'Monsieur Hire.' Rogerebert.com, 21 December 2012. Accessed at www.rogerebert.com/reviews/great-movie-monsieur-hire-1989 on 26 January 2018.
Ellis-Petersen, Hannah. 'Decaying East London Tower Block to House 12-hour Macbeth Production.' *The Guardian*, 19 June 2014.
Etchells, Tim. *Certain Fragments: Contemporary Performance and Forced Entertainment*. London: Routledge, 1999.
——. 'Taking Time.' Nachtkritik.de, 22 June 2015a. Accessed at https://www.nachtkritik.de/index.php?option=com_content&view=article&id=11138 on 26 January 2018.
——. 'Table Top Shakespeare: Nowhere to run, nowhere to hide.' Exeuntmagazine.com, 2 July 2015b. Accessed at http://exeuntmagazine.com/features/table-top-tim-etchells/ on 26 January 2018.
Ewert, Kevin. 'A Midsummer Night's Dream (As You Like It).' Review. *Shakespeare Bulletin*, Vol. 31, No. 4, Winter 2013. 746–49.
'Federay'. 'Ad Lib or Not Ad Lib.' September 2008. Accessed at http://thefactory.wikifoundry.com/page/Ad+Lib+or+Not+Ad+Lib on 26 January 2018.
Frere-Jones, Sasha. 'Ambient Genius: The Working Life of Brian Eno.' *The New Yorker*, 7 July 2014.
Giannachi, Gabriella and Mary Luckhurst, eds. *On Directing: Interviews with Directors*. New York: St. Martin's, 1999.
Graham, Scott and Steven Hoggett. *The Frantic Assembly Book of Devising Theatre*. Second Edition. New York: Routledge, 2014.
Harvie, Jen and Andy Lavender, eds. *Making Contemporary Theatre: International Rehearsal Processes*. Manchester: Manchester University Press, 2010.
Haydon, Andrew. 'Postdramatic theatre is no longer a closed book.' *The Guardian*, 11 November 2008.
Healy, Patrick. 'Two Versions of 'Twelfth Night' Coming From Bedlam Theater Troupe.' *The New York Times*, 4 February 2015. Accessed at https://artsbeat.blogs.nytimes.com/2015/02/04/two-versions-of-twelfth-night-coming-from-bedlam-theater-troupe/ on 26 January 2018.

Heddon, Deirdre and Jane Milling. *Devising Performance: A Critical History*. New York: Palgrave Macmillan, 2006.
Innes, Christopher and Maria Shevtsova. *The Cambridge Introduction to Theatre Directing*. Cambridge: Cambridge University Press, 2013.
Isherwood, Charles. 'In Praise of Repertory Theater: Macbeth at the Matinee, Miller at Night.' *The New York Times*, 11 August 2016.
Knight, G. Wilson. *Principles of Shakespearian Production*. London: Faber and Faber, 1936.
Lehmann, Hans-Thies. *Postdramatic Theatre*, translated by Karen Jurs-Munby. New York: Routledge, 2006 (German edition 1999).
Love, Catherine. 'Keeping the Secret.' Exeuntmagazine.com, 19 September 2013. Accessed at http://exeuntmagazine.com/features/keeping-the-secret on 26 January 2018.
Lynn, Kirk. *Fixing King John*. Unpublished script supplied by the author.
Mamet, David. *True and False. Heresy and Common Sense for the Actor*. New York: Vintage Books, 1999.
——. *Theatre*. New York: Faber and Faber, 2010.
Mazer, Cary. 'Not Not Shakespeare: Directorial Adaptation, Authorship, and Ownership.' *Shakespeare Bulletin*, Vol. 23, No. 3, Fall 2005. 23–42.
McCabe, Terry. *Mis-directing the Play: An Argument Against Contemporary Theatre*. Chicago: Ivan R. Dee, 2001.
Mitchell, Katie. *The Director's Craft*. New York: Routledge, 2009.
Mitter, Shomit. *Systems of Rehearsal: Stanislavsky, Brecht, Grotowski and Brook*. London: Routledge, 1992.
Mitter, Shomit and Maria Shevtsova, eds. *Fifty Key Theatre Directors*. New York: Routledge, 2005.
Novek, Loren. 'The Implosion Model.' Exeuntmagazine.com, 6 March 2015. Accessed at http://exeuntmagazine.com/features/the-implosion-model/ on 26 January 2018.
O'Connor, Donal. 'It's Carroll's third time directing lead character Tom McCamus.' *The Stratford Beacon Herald*, 1 June 2014.
O'Kane, Josh. 'Stewart Copeland on going from the rock world to classical music.' *The Globe and Mail*, 19 May 2015.
Prescott, Paul. 'Year of Shakespeare: Troilus and Cressida (RSC).' Bloggingshakespeare .com, 6 September 2012. Accessed at http://bloggingshakespeare.com/year-of-shakespeare-troilus-and-cressida-rsc on 26 January 2018.
Radosavljevic, Duska. *The Contemporary Ensemble: Interviews with Theatre-Makers*. New York: Routledge, 2013.
Roose-Evans, James. *Experimental Theatre from Stanislavsky to Peter Brook*. Fourth Edition revised and updated. London: Routledge, 1989.
Russell, Mark. 'Regarding Performance Theatre Today.' *Pew Fellowships in the Arts Newsletter*, Spring/Summer 2004.
Schafer, Elizabeth. *Ms-Directing Shakespeare: Women Direct Shakespeare*. London: The Women's Press, 1998.
Shalwitz, Howard. 'Theatrical Innovation: Whose Job Is It?' Address to National Conference of the Theatre Communications Guild, Boston MA, 21 June 2012. Accessed at http://www.tcgcircle.org/2012/07/theatrical-innovation-whose-job-is-it/ on 26 January 2018.
Shepherd, Simon. *Direction*. New York: Palgrave Macmillan, 2012.

Shevtsova, Maria and Christopher Innes. *Directors/Directing: Conversations on Theatre*. Cambridge: Cambridge University Press, 2009.
Sidiropoulou, Avra. *Authoring Performance: The Director in Contemporary Theatre*. New York: Palgrave Macmillan, 2011.
Stanislavski, Konstantin. *An Actor's Work on a Role*, translated by Jean Benedetti. New York: Routledge, 2010.
Tannahill, Jordan. *Theatre of the Unimpressed: In Search of Vital Drama*. Toronto: Coach House Books, 2015.
Williams, Raymond. *Drama in Performance*. Buckingham: Open University Press, 1991 (originally published in revised version 1968).
Worthen, W.B. *Shakespeare and the Authority of Performance*. Cambridge: Cambridge University Press, 1997.
——. 'Intoxicating Rhythms: Or, Shakespeare, Literary Drama, and Performance (Studies).' *Shakespeare Quarterly*, Vol. 62, No. 3, Fall 2001. 309–39.

# Index

13P (playwright's collective), 28

Abrahams, Chris, 92
Adassinsky, Anton, 44
Alexander, Bill, 94
Alguire, Jeff, 118
American Conservatory Theater, 61
*Angela's Ashes*, 126
Antoine, Andre, 23
Aristotle, 14, 20, 32, 34–5, 37
Arnold, Jade, 114–15, 117
Artaud, Anton, 31–3, 35
*As You Like It*, 92–3
*Atanarjuat: The Fast Runner*, 81
Auster, David, 54–60

Baker, Annie, 138, 141
Bassett, Alexandra, 134, 136–9
Beale, Simon Russell, 13, 62
Beatty, Warren, 81
Beckett, Samuel, 28
Bedlam (theatre company), 1
Beier, Karin, 13
Billington, Michael, 7, 10, 14
Bogart, Anne, 12, 29–30, 41, 46–7, 82–3, 88, 104, 115
Bogdanov, Michael, 65–6, 93
Botusov, Yuri, 43
Brecht, Bertolt, 32–4, 39, 77
Brody, Richard, 72
Brook, Peter, 2, 58, 89
Builder's Association, The, 39
Burton, Richard, 81

Calarco, Joe, 94
Carbone 14, 6–7
Carroll, Tim, 101–5, 121–2
Cave, Nick, 11
*Celebration (Festen)*, 107
Chavkin, Rachel, 142
Cheek By Jowl, 92–3
Chekhov, Anton, 23, 83

Chicago Shakespeare Theater, 64, 94
Chronegk, Ludwig, 23
Churchill, Caryl, 12
Cimolino, Antoni, 55, 59, 61
Clapp, Susannah, 93
Collins, John, 40
Complicite, 40, 113
Composition, 29–30, 40–41, 47
Conlogue, Ray, 6–9
Copeland, Stewart, 46
Cowie, Andrew, 5, 7–10
Creation Theatre, 140
Crimp, Martin, 37
*Cry Trojans! (Troilus and Cressida)*, 81–2
*Cymbeline*, 13–14, 44–5

Darlington, Madge, 134, 139
Darwin, Charles, 23
Davis, Will, 142
Delappe, Sarah, 138
Derevo, 44
*Desdemona: A Play About a Handkerchief*, 96
devising, devised theatre, 8–9, 30, 34, 37, 39, 41–3, 45, 53–4, 58, 70, 80–90, 91–2, 105, 122, 127–8, 135, 139, 142–3
Dietz, Steven, 24
Dionisotti, Paola, 94
Dodin, Lev, 5
Donmar Warehouse, 26, 93
Douthit, Lou, 95–7

Elevator Repair Service, 40
English Shakespeare Company, 64–6
Eno, Brian, 46
Etchells, Tim, 41, 70–71
Eugene O'Neill Theater Center/National Theatre Institute, 45–6

Factory, The, 102–5, 121–2
*Far Away*, 12–13

152

*Fixing King John*, 98–100, 105, 127, 141
*Fixing Timon of Athens*, 100
Forced Entertainment, 33, 40–41, 61–2, 69–71, 73, 76, 142
framing devices, 72, 92–4, 101

Gielgud, John, 111
Globe Theatre, 101–2, 139–40
Gob Squad, 33, 61, 142
Gold, Sam, 138, 141
Grandage, Michael, 26–7

Hadden, John, 137
Hall, Edward, 64
*Hamlet*, 8, 21, 64, 81, 102–3, 106, 121, 137
Harvie, Jen, 38–42, 143
Haydon, Andrew, 33
*Henry IV Parts One and Two*, 65–6
*Henry V*, 11–12, 64, 66, 71–9
*Henry 5 Live From Times Square*, 73–80, 127
*Henrys, The*, 65–7
*hmlt*, 83, 107–23
Holloway-Burrell, JaMeeka, 114
Hove, Ivo van, 66–7
Hytner, Nick, 72–3

Ibsen, Henrik, 23
Improvised Shakespeare Company, 123
interpreting/interpretation, directing as, 7–12, 21, 24, 26–7, 38, 43–5, 47, 51, 62, 78, 81, 97, 103–5, 128–9, 137, 139, 142
Isherwood, Charles, 60–61

Jagodowski, TJ, 2–4, 41
Joseph, Melanie, 134
*Julius Caesar*, 12

Kane, Sarah, 37
Karpovsky, Alex, 3
Kauffman, Annie, 134
Kazan, Elia, 81
*King John*, 99–102, 105, 127
*King Lear*, 100–101, 127–9, 136
Kissane, Tamara, 84–7, 89, 114
Kneehigh, 44–5
Kunuk, Zacharias, 81

LaBute, Neil, 94
Landau, Tina, 29–30, 82–3
Lavender, Andy, 38–42, 143
*LEAR*, 96, 107, 127–9
LeCompte, Elizabeth, 4, 43–4, 81
Leconte, Patrice, 10–11, 60
Lee, Young Jean, 96, 127–8, 138, 141
Lehmann, Hans-Thies, 33–9, 42, 77, 83, 88
Leonard, Luke, 134
Lepage, Robert, 2, 5, 41
Lesley, Lana, 134–5, 137–8
Little Green Pig Theatrical Concern, 40, 83–90, 107–22, 127
Lloyd, Phyllida, 93
Love, Catherine, 9–10
*Love's Labour's Lost*, 140
Lucidity Suitcase Intercontinental, 73
Lynn, Kirk, 99–101, 134–43
Lyric Hammersmith Secret Theatre, 9–10

*Macbeth*, 64, 68
*Maccountant*, 83
Maheu, Gilles, 6–7, 9
Mallarino, Tatiana, 80
Maly Theatre, 5
Mamet, David, 20–21, 89
Marks, Dana, 84, 109, 113–14
Materic, Mladen, 5
Maxwell, Robert, 40
Mazer, Cary, 94
McBurney, Simon, 40
McCabe, Terry, 89
McCourt, Frank, 126
McDonagh, Martin, 83
*Measure for Measure*, 27, 71
Mee, Chuck, 37
Mendes, Sam, 13
*Merchant of Venice, The*, 101
"mickey mousing", 35, 142–3
*Midsummer Night's Dream, A*, 58, 92–3, 107, 123–7, 140
Miller, Jason, 54–6, 59–60
Moscow Art Theatre, 23
Muller, Heiner, 6–8

National Theatre, 62, 72–3
naturalism, 22–3, 34

Nawras, Joshua, 68
Nemirovich-Danchenko, Vladimir, 23
Neugebauer, Lila, 138
New Works Festival, Pittsburgh, 106

O'Berski, Jaybird, 84–8, 90, 106–8, 112, 114–5, 119, 121
O'Connell, Patrick, 65
obstructions, 41–2, 102, 104, 106, 121–2
Oliver, Dan, 113
Open Stage (former Yugoslavia), 5
Oregon Shakespeare Festival, 94–7
Original Practices, 101, 108, 119, 121, 127, 137, 140, 142

Pankov, Vladimir, 7
Pasquesi, David, 2–4, 41
*Patton*, 76
Pearl, Katie, 134
Pennington, Michael, 65
Perceval, Luk, 41–2
Perloff, Carey, 61
Phillips, Robin, 13
Phillips, Thaddeus, 40, 74–8, 80, 127
*pieces bien fait*, 24
Pig Iron, 45–6, 142
*Pillowman, The*, 83
Play on!, 94–100
postdramatic theatre, 30, 33–8, 42, 51, 77, 88
Prescott, Paul, 5, 7–9
Pryce, Jonathan, 93
Punchdrunk, 67–8
Purgar-McDonald, Marleigh, 117

Radosavljevic, Duska, 38, 42–5
Ravenhill, Mark, 4
realism, 14, 22–5, 30, 32–4, 38, 51, 72–3, 78–9, 114, 119, 127
Rice, Emma, 45, 140
*Richard II*, 65, 83–5
Richie, 64, 83–90, 95, 106, 127
RIFT, 68
*Roman Tragedies*, 64, 66–7
*Romeo and Juliet*, 13, 94, 101
Rothenberg, Dan, 45
Rourke, Josie, 94

Royal Shakespeare Company, 4–5, 7–9, 62, 64, 81–2, 138–9, 141
Rude Mechs, 46, 61, 97–8, 100–101, 105, 127, 133–43
Russell, Beth, 55–6
Russell, Mark, 77–8
Rylance, Mark, 101

Sale, Courtney, 134
Saxe-Meiningen, Georg II Duke of, 23
Scott, George C., 76
Scribe, Eugene, 24
*Sesame Street*, 127–9
Shakespeare & Company, 138
Shakespeare at Winedale, 137
*Shakespeare's R&J*, 94
Shalwitz, Howard, 51–3, 62
*Shipment, The*, 127
Sides, Shawn, 134–5, 137–9, 141
Simon, Josette, 141
SITI Company, 29, 61–2
*Sleep No More*, 67, 138
*Splendor in the Grass*, 81
Stanislavski, Konstantin, 23, 125–6
Stratford Festival, Ontario, 54–62, 100–102

*Taming of the Shrew, The*, 93–4, 137
Tannahill, Jordan, 26, 28, 142
tasks, task-setting, 11, 30, 35, 39–40, 42, 70, 80–82, 84–5, 87–90, 101–2, 104–6, 122, 127, 129
*Tempest, The*, 13
Theatre Libre, 23
*Timon of Athens*, 71
Tompa, Gabor, 42–3
Toneelgroep Amsterdam, 64, 66–7
*Troilus and Cressida*, 4–5, 7–9, 81
*Trust Us, This Is All Made Up*, 2–4
Tucker, Eric, 1
*Twelfth Night*, 140

Unseam'd Shakespeare Company, 52–4, 68
*Untitled Feminist Show*, 127

Viewpoints, 29–30, 47, 70, 82, 109, 119, 121
Vogel, Paula, 96

*Wars of the Roses* (ESC), 64–5
Watts, Reggie, 112
Weems, Marianne, 39
"well made plays", 24, 28, 32
Wells, Caitlin, 114, 116
Williams, Robin, 117
Wolf, Dale, 109, 115
Wood, Natalie, 81
Woodvine, John, 66

Wooly Mammoth, 51, 62
Wooster Group, The, 4–5, 7–10, 33, 43, 61, 81–2, 118
World Stage Festival, Harbourfront, Toronto, 5–6

Yarovaya, Elena, 44

Zola, Emile, 22–3